The Philosophical Approach to God

W. NORRIS CLARKE, S.J.

The Philosophical Approach to God

A New Thomistic Perspective

Second Revised Edition

Fordham University Press

New York 2007

Library of Congress Cataloging-in-Publication Data

Clarke, W. Norris (William Norris), 1915–
The philosophical approach to God : a new Thomistic perspective / W. Norris
Clarke.—2nd rev. ed.
    p. cm.
Includes bibliographical references.
ISBN-13: 978-0-8232-2719-8 (pbk. : alk. paper)
ISBN-10: 0-8232-2719-7 (pbk. : alk. paper)
    1. God (Christianity) 2. Neo-Scholasticism. I. Title.
BT103.C53 2007
231—dc22

                                   2007001817

Printed in the United States of America
09 08 07   5 4 3 2 1
Second edition
First edition published by Wake Forest University, 1979.

CONTENTS

FOREWORD TO SECOND REVISED EDITION

In 1978 I was invited to be the main speaker at the annual James Montgomery Hester Seminar at Wake Forest University, dedicated to the continuing dialogue between the two great intellectual approaches of the human mind to God, one through philosophical reason, through the Book of Nature, the other through faith and theological reason from the Book of Revelation. I have selected here for reprinting from the larger seminar the three lectures I gave, which focus on the ascent to God by philosophical reason in the Neo-Thomist tradition of "creative retrieval" of St. Thomas Aquinas.

The first two lectures deal with my adaptation of the resources of the Thomistic approach: the first through the more recent turn to the Inner Path through "the unrestricted dynamism of the human spirit toward God" as the infinite fullness of Being: through the intellect toward the fullness of Being as Truth, and through the will toward the fullness of Being as Good, as lovable. The second lecture deals with the classic Thomistic metaphysical ascent from creatures to God through participation and finitude. Note that the strict "path" of ascent is not that of the better known "Five Ways." The latter, St. Thomas claims, is meant for beginners, and always starts from some evident sense experience. But only the Fourth goes all the way to conclude to a single infinite Source of all being. This conclusion occurs much later in the *Summa Theologiae* (Part I, Question 11, Article 3), where Thomas speaks of it as "And this is God," not just as "And this is what all men call God." The arguments I will present here start with a brief reconstruction of a more adequate synthesis of the Five Ways, using participation metaphysics only for the last part, the passage to a single infinite Source of all being. Then I present a more strictly metaphysical argument starting from within Aquinas's Neoplatonic participation metaphysics.

The third lecture deals with the question of whether the conception of God in the contemporary Whiteheadian Process Philosophy is really compatible with that of Christianity, in particular that of Catholic Christianity as represented by St. Thomas. My answer is principally negative, but with indications of openings for future fruitful dialogue. The original edition of this book had a very limited printing, has been long out of print, and many scholars have asked me to have it reprinted. Since the original publisher, Wake Forest University Press, is no longer in operation, and since most of the content seems as relevant today as in 1979, Fordham University Press has graciously agreed to reprint this work of its own long-time Fordham professor.

I have taken the opportunity to make significant revisions of the original text, especially in the second and third lectures, so that this is properly a "second revised edition."

W. Norris Clarke, S.J.
Fordham University
Bronx, New York

PART ONE

The Turn to the Inner Way in Contemporary Neo-Thomism

Recent History of Thomism

The aim of the first three chapters, which constitute part I of this monograph, is to present for your reflection and discussion some of the significant ongoing developments in the contemporary Neo-Thomist school of philosophers and philosophizing theologians with respect to the philosophical approach to God.

I understand the term "Neo-Thomist" here very broadly to signify that loosely but recognizably united group of thinkers who acknowledge that the basic inspiration and structure of their thought derives from St. Thomas Aquinas, even though each one may have made various creative adaptations of his own, in both method and content, inspired by various movements of thought since the time of St. Thomas. Many of you may perhaps believe that since the heyday of Jacques Maritain and Etienne Gilson, when it seemed temporarily to regain a place in the sun in contemporary thought, Thomism had quietly faded away, save perhaps in a few seminaries. Others may perhaps wish that it would just fade away and cease to bother us, once and for all, as anything but a chapter in the history of thought. Neither belief nor wish seems likely of immediate fulfillment. Thomism has a remarkable survival power, and every so often, just when it seems that it is about to fade out, it has a way of renewing itself, like the phoenix, usually by a double movement of deeper return to its own sources plus the creative assimilation of some new insight or method of later thought.

This pattern of rise, decline, and renewal has been played out in Thomism during roughly the second and third quarters of the twentieth century.[1] During the first half of the century there was a strong Thomistic revival in the community of Catholic thought and educational institutions, sparked by the famous encyclical letter *Aeterni Patris* of Pope Leo XIII in 1879, which initiated the Thomistic revival in Europe. This was the period of Thomistic "triumphalism" in the American Catholic world, as we who grew up under it and now look back upon it have come to call it. Church leaders exerted strong authoritarian pressure to make St. Thomas the "common doctor," the major guide and norm of sound teaching in both philosophy and theology for Catholic educational institutions, inspired by Pope Leo's characterization of the synthesis of St. Thomas as "the best way of philosophizing" (*optima ratio philosophandi*) and his recommendation that it replace all other methods and doctrines of philosophy and theology in the formation of the Church's priests. During that time, if one went to any Catholic college or university or seminary—save for a few rather lonesome Franciscan enclaves—it was a matter of course that the basic training in philosophy, as well as theology, would be some brand of Thomism. This was the establishment orthodoxy of the time.

Somewhere in the late 1950s and 1960s, however, the whole movement went into a rapid and precipitous decline. It is not entirely clear whether this was due to a revolt against the authoritarian aura surrounding Thomistic teaching, the overconfidently dogmatic attitude of too many Thomists, the Second Vatican Council with its new opening to modern thought, the general turning away in the philosophical world from the great system-building philosophers of the past, the pull of new philosophical schools coming into the limelight—such as existentialism, personalism, phenomenology, and especially existential phenomenology among young Catholic scholars—or a combination of all these forces. The fact remains that young Catholic philosophers just simply went elsewhere than to Thomistic sources and centers for their training, and this was quickly reflected in their classroom teaching. It is not that they carefully studied St. Thomas first, then rejected him. They simply lost interest and commitment and moved elsewhere.

As a result, the chances now seem to me considerably less than fifty/ fifty—and almost nil in some places—that if one goes to a Catholic college or university today he will be exposed to a basic Thomistic training in philosophy. The whole authoritarian pressure to impose St. Thomas as the established master has collapsed. One benefit of this is that it is now possible at last to approach him on his own merits as a thinker. Students no longer have to fight him as an authority-figure; most know and hear too little about him even to know what they would be fighting against or why. As a result, when students do come into contact with St. Thomas, they can now approach him with a whole fresh attitude, discovering him as a thinker in his own right and not as imposed from above by some other authority-figure. This is what is in fact happening, it seems; there is a quietly growing renewed interest in the thought of St. Thomas, especially his philosophy, for its own sake, among both Catholics and non-Catholics.

The Transcendental Thomist Movement

In this quiet renewal of Thomistic thought, one of the movements that has attracted the most interest and shown the most creative power in synthesizing old with new goes by the loose general title of "Transcendental Thomism."[2]

It was initiated by the Belgian Jesuit philosopher Joseph Maréchal, in the late 1920s and 1930s at Louvain, in his famous five-volume work *Point de départ de la métaphysique*. In his work, Maréchal went in the door of the Kantian method of transcendental analysis to discover the existence of God as the necessary *a priori* condition of the dynamism of human intelligence. This approach ran into considerable opposition from the contemporary Thomist establishment because of its supposedly dangerous affinities with German idealist thought in taking over the Kantian transcendental method—which, rather than moving directly outward to examine the objective

3

contents of man's knowledge about the world, turns inward to search out the necessary *a priori* conditions of possibility of the inner life of the human spirit in its activities of thinking and willing, and which studies the dynamic structure, the form rather than the content, of human thinking.

Nonetheless, the essentials of Maréchal's method and its results have since been taken up by many contemporary disciples in various countries, each of whom tends to put his own unique and original stamp on it. Thus we have Karl Rahner and Johannes Lotz in Germany; Emerich Coreth in Austria;[3] in France, André Marc (my own first professor of metaphysics, now deceased) and Joseph de Finance (preceded a quarter of a century before by Maurice Blondel, who in his famous first edition of *L'Action* in 1893, prior even to Maréchal, applied the transcendental method to the dynamism of the will); Bernard Lonergan in Canada and then the United States, with his own quite original development of the same basic orientation;[4] and Joseph Donceel,[5] originally a student of Maréchal's in Belgium but for many years Professor at Fordham University in the United States—all the above, of course, with their various groups of less well-known disciples. I might add that, though not considered a fully orthodox card-carrying member of the school, I am still a deeply sympathetic fellow-traveler. It is a remarkable fact that all of the above—though not their disciples—are Jesuit thinkers, either philosophers or theologians or both, so that Transcendental Thomism might well be said to be the most characteristic movement among Jesuit Thomists in the last half of the twentieth century.

How do I differ from the strict Transcendental Thomist position? I accept the ascent to God through the dynamism of intellect and will, but not the roundabout way of grounding the validity of human knowledge by first going up through God as final cause, then back to our ordinary knowledge of the finite world of our experience. I have been told, by those who have studied the later correspondence of Maréchal, that he himself admitted he had done that only because he wanted to go in the Kantian door to bring his readers out the Thomistic door. Otherwise a more direct Thomistic path was quite valid.

The movement is by no means accepted as an authentic development of Thomism by all Thomists today, however. Many thinkers among the Dominican order, and especially the descendants of the older Maritain and Gilson schools, are quite critical and suspicious that it leans too much toward idealism or overstresses the subjective dimensions of human thought, underplaying the objective causal metaphysics that has always been the hallmark of Thomism.[6] Nonetheless, the movement has shown itself to be remarkably creative and dynamic, forming a basis for the immensely rich and influential philosophical-theological synthesis of Karl Rahner and his school.[7] Hence I think it is well worth presenting to you here, though I have no intention of surveying the positions of these various authors in detail. What I intend to do is rather to extract what seems to me the essential core common to the whole school and present it in a way that I myself can accept and use in constructing a viable philosophical approach to God—one that is quite free, it seems to me, of any leanings toward idealism or of underplaying the objective causal metaphysics that is indeed an integral part of authentic Thomism.

Paul Tillich's Criticism of Traditional Thomism

I would like to take as my starting point of reference a famous essay by Paul Tillich, the distinguished Protestant philosopher-theologian—an essay which I am sure that most of you at Wake Forest University, more at home as I presume you are in the theological tradition of Protestant Christianity, are familiar with and which has probably colored no little your own attitudes toward St. Thomas. This is his essay on "Two Types of Philosophy of Religion," which first appeared in the *Union Seminary Quarterly* in May 1946 and has since been reprinted in the collection of Tillich's essays, *Theology of Culture* (Oxford University Press, 1959).

In his essay, Tillich distinguishes two main types of philosophical approach to God inherited from medieval thought. One is the Augustinian-Franciscan school represented by Augustine, Anselm, and Bonaventure, with which Tillich himself is deeply sympathetic and which has inspired his own thought. The other is the Aristotelian-Thomistic tradition, toward which he feels quite out of sympathy and critical. The essence of the first approach is that God is found by turning within to the inner life of the human spirit, where He is discovered to be one who is always already present as the necessary ultimate ground of the inner life of thought and love, but whose presence is veiled at first, not yet recognized by us. This discovery proceeds both along the line of intelligence, through the notion of Infinite Being as the hidden light through which we know all finite being, and along the line of will, through the notion of the Infinite Good, the ultimate drawing power or goal through which we desire all finite goods. The process is always the same in its various modalities: the unveiling to explicit knowledge and love of the God who is already God-with-us, the inner light and guide of the life of the spirit, but not yet recognized as such. The discovery of God is an interior journey into our own depths, not a journey outward to find God at the other end of the material cosmos.

St. Thomas, on the other hand, Tillich characterizes as the first "atheist" (implicit, of course) in Christian thought, the consistent following out of whose principles and methods leads inexorably to our modem secular experience of the absence of God, the death of God. The reason is that St. Thomas's method, following Aristotle in his famous Prime Mover argument, is to seek to *demonstrate* the existence of God in a rigorous scientific way by starting from the external material cosmos outside the human soul itself, discovering how its being is deficient in some way, not self-explanatory, and then, at the end of a long chain of premises, finally concluding to God as the Ultimate First Cause of the data we started with. But the radical vice of this procedure—and all similar ones, logically valid or not—is that it begins by treating God as the Absent One, absent both from ourselves and the world at the beginning of the proof and finally logically concluded to at the end of the proof.

Yet to start off treating God as the Absent One, as a God who is not God-with-us but outside us somewhere, to be sought by a journey through the cosmos, is the essence of the atheistic attitude—or at least the first decisive step toward it. If God is not present with us, in us, from the beginning, and somehow recognized as such, we shall never find Him. In fact, it took a long time for the latent atheism of this method to be revealed in its true colors. But once modern science and the philosophy inspired by it rejected the intermediary steps in the logical journey to God through the natural cosmos, we woke up to the traumatic realization that the absent God could no longer be found at all. We were full into the secular-minded absence-of-God mentality which is dominant today.

This is indeed in many ways a tendentious interpretation of St. Thomas, who was clearly a deeply believing Christian and who experienced God as immediately present through grace, even through direct mystical experience. But coming as he did in the middle of the sudden massive influx of the new Aristotelian science and philosophy, St. Thomas felt that his immediate task in the service of God and the Church was to show how even through this new logical-scientific method and philosophy of nature one could also reach God—through reason as a preparation for revelation, and with what appeared to be greater logical rigor and conceptual precision than in the older, more intuitive and subjective interior approach. Identifying St. Thomas too exclusively with Aristotle, as Tillich tends to do, does not do justice to the rich Neoplatonic dimension of his metaphysics, which proceeds much more from the veiled presence of God revealed through the participated perfection of His creatures than is the case with the Aristotelian arguments from motion.

Nonetheless, there is a great deal of insight and not a little disturbing truth in the basic message of Tillich's essay. There is a perennial strength and resonance with the depths of the human spirit in the Augustinian-Franciscan interior approach that somehow seems missing in the more rigorously argued cosmic path initiated by Aristotle, even developed and enriched as it was by St. Thomas. It is precisely in its effort to fill this gap in Thomistic thought that the special historical significance of the Transcendental Thomist movement seems to me to lie. It represents a new turn to the inner path, analogous to that in the Augustinian tradition, but discovered within the resources of St. Thomas's own thought and his more rigorous philosophical method—although he himself, aside from a few pregnant hints, never explicitly exploited these resources in the same way.

Discovery of God through the Dynamism of the Human Spirit

The Transcendental Thomists did not come to discover this inner path under the stimulus of Tillich's criticism, since they had already begun to publish in the late 1920s, but rather under the challenge of the Kantian critique, with its new transcendental method so powerfully exploited not only by Kant but also by Fichte, Hegel, and the later Neo-Kantian schools in Europe. For the Kantian critique of knowledge and metaphysics still dominated European philosophical thought in the early twentieth century, and had in fact proved the principal challenge to the rising Neo-Thomist revival, which it accused of a naive and uncritical confidence in the mind's ability to know extra-mental reality. But it is a remarkable fact that in returning to St. Thomas to find resources to meet the contemporary challenge of the Kantian critique, the Transcendental Thomists rejoined in a new way the old Augustinian inner way to God, thus filling a disturbing lacuna in St. Thomas's own metaphysical achievement.

The essence of the Transcendental Thomist approach to God seems to me to be this: it has brought out of obscurity into full development St. Thomas's own profound doctrine of the dynamism of the human spirit, both as intellect and will, toward the Infinite—a dynamism inscribed in the very nature of man as *a priori* condition of possibility of both his knowing and his willing activities—and then applied this doctrine to ground epistemology, philosophical anthropology, metaphysics, and the flowering of the latter into natural theology. Using this radical dynamism of the human spirit to illuminate the foundations of the whole of Thomistic philosophy—in particular the rational ascent to God—was entirely in harmony with St. Thomas's own deepest thought. For he himself had worked out quite explicitly and carefully, in his treatise on the ethical life of man, the doctrine of the natural desire in man for the beatific vision of God. Yet intent as he was on following out the new Aristotelian cosmological approach in metaphysics through the objective framework of act and potency, he never seems to have thought of using the doctrine as a key piece in the formal structural development of epistemology or metaphysics, including natural theology. He devoted his explicit efforts toward applying this spiritual dynamism to work out the objective intellectual comprehension of the world itself, including man, rather than toward developing in detail the *a priori* transcendental conditions of possibility of the operation of the mind itself—although even here, certain basic seminal positions are laid down whose fecundity needs only to be unfolded.

This is what the Transcendental Thomists have done in their analysis of the transcendental conditions of possibility of human knowing and willing. Let me now present briefly the essential core of this analysis, insofar as I myself can take philosophical responsibility for it and make it my own.

The Ascent through the Dynamism of the Intellect

As we reflect on the activities of our intellectual knowing power, we come to recognize it as an inexhaustible dynamism of inquiry, ever searching to lay hold more deeply and widely on the universe of reality. It is impossible to restrict its horizon of inquiry to any limited area of reality, to any goal short of all that there is to know about all that there is. For our experience of knowing reveals to us that each time we come to know some new object or aspect of reality we rest in it at first, savoring and exploring its intelligibility as far as we can. But as soon as we run up against its limits and discover that it is finite, the mind at once rebounds farther, reaching beyond it to wherever else it leads, to whatever else there is to be known beyond it. This process continues indefinitely in ever-expanding and ever-deepening circles. As we reflect on the significance of this inexhaustible and unquenchable drive toward the fullness of all there is to know, we realize that the only adequate goal of our dynamism of knowing is the totality of all being. We live mentally, therefore, as they express it, in "the horizon of being"—or, as St. Thomas himself puts it in his own technical terminology, the only adequate formal object of the human mind is being itself.

This means that the mind must have a dynamic *a priori* orientation, an aptitude or affinity, for all that is, for the totality of being—an aptitude that constitutes it precisely as a knowing nature in the intellectual and not merely the sensible order. Now every dynamism or active potency, St. Thomas holds, has its goal already inscribed in it in some way, in the mode of final cause, as that toward which it naturally tends, as that which naturally attracts or draws it to itself, and therefore as that which is somehow already present to it. In a dynamism which is as self-aware as ours is—aware not only of the contents of its knowledge, but also of its own activity of knowing and radical desire to know—there must accordingly be a dim, obscure, implicit, but nonetheless real awareness of this goal as drawing it.

This means that the mind has, from its first conscious movement from emptiness toward fulfillment, a kind of implicit, pre-conceptual, anticipatory grasp or foretaste of being as the encompassing horizon and goal of all its inquiries. As Karl Rahner and the Germans like to put it, this is not a *Begriff* (i.e., an explicit, thematized concept or distinct idea of being); it is rather a *Vorgriff* (i.e., a pre-conceptual, implicit, unthematized, anticipatory awareness of being present to the mind as its goal, as its connatural good drawing it). This is to live mentally within the horizon of being. It is because of this innate *a priori* orientation that all our questions are directed toward being: "*Is* this the case? What *is* this? How *is* it?" All the answers, too, to our determinate inquiries are framed against the background of being. All our judgments reflect, at least implicitly, this insertion of our knowledge into the horizon of being. The "is" of being is the hidden backdrop and frame of all our assertions. We continually say, "This *is*, that *is*, this *is* such and such," and by so doing we insert some limited essence or aspect of the real in its place in the whole of being. Thus we assert implicitly the participation of all finite essences or modes of being in the ultimate, all-pervasive attribute of all things, the very act of presence or existence itself, expressed by the inconspicuous but omnipresent "is" that in some equivalent way is the inner form of all human judgments.

This *a priori* orientation toward being—with its implicit pre-conceptual awareness of being by connatural affinity and desire, as we know a good by being drawn to it—is a genuine *a priori* presence of being to the human mind constitutive of its very nature as a dynamic faculty. It is not, however, a Cartesian innate idea, since it is not present as a clear and distinct conceptual content, and takes a long experience of conscious, reflective knowing before it can emerge into explicit conscious awareness expressible in conceptual form. The entire mental life of man consists in gradually filling in this at first conceptually empty and indeterminate but limitless horizon of being with increasingly determinate conceptual comprehension, as we step by step come to know one part of this totality after another.

Let us further analyze this vague and indeterminate horizon of being which defines ahead of time the whole enterprise of human knowing and is present to it in an implicit, pre-conceptual lived awareness, as a connatural attracting goal, from the first breath of intellectual life.

The first point we notice is that no limits can be set to this field of intentionality, this anticipated horizon of being. Any attempt to do so immediately stimulates the mind to leap beyond these limits in intentional thrust and desire. Thus this horizon or totality of being-to-be-known appears at first as an indefinite, indeterminate, but unlimited and illimitable field, a field to which no determinate limits can be set.

What is the actual content of this field? There are only two alternatives. If the actual content of being is nothing but an endless or indefinite field of all *finite* entities or intelligible structures, the dynamism of the mind is doomed to endless rebounding from one finite to another, with no final satisfaction or unqualified fulfillment ever attainable, or even possible. Our restless, unquenchable search has no actually existing final goal. It trails off endlessly into ever-receding, always finite horizons, its inexhaustible abyss of longing and capacity ever unfilled and in principle unfillable. Once we postulate that this situation is definitive and cannot be overcome—that there is no proportion between the depths of our capacity, the reach of our mind, and what there is for it actually to grasp—the very possibility arouses a profound metaphysical restlessness and sadness within us; the dynamism of our mind turns out to be a strange existential surd, an anomaly. It is a dynamism ordered precisely toward a non-existent goal; a drive through all finites toward nothing; an innate, inextinguishable summons to frustration: a living absurdity. Sartre would indeed be right, when he says every human being longs for the infinite, but since God is dead, "man is a useless passion."

The other possibility is that somewhere hidden within this unlimited horizon of being there exists an actually infinite Plenitude of Being, in which all other beings participate yet of which they are but imperfect images. St. Thomas describes this actually Infinite Plenitude not as a particular being—with its connotation of determinate limits setting it apart from other equally finite beings—but rather as the pure subsistent plenitude of be-ing, of the act of existence itself, *Ipsum Esse Subsistens*, pure subsistent to-be. It now becomes the adequate, totally fulfilling goal of the dynamism of our minds, matching superabundantly the inexhaustible abyss of our own capacity and desire to know: one abyss, a negative one, calling out to another, a positive one. As the German mystical poet Angelus Silesius so beautifully put it, "The abyss in me calls out to the abyss in God. Tell me, which is deeper?" The existence of this Infinite Center of being (obviously it would have to be *actually existent*, for if it were merely possible, nothing else could bring it into existence and it would be in fact impossible) now gives full intelligibility to the horizon of being itself, as its unifying center and source, and also confers full and magnificent intelligibility on the natural dynamism of my mind and the whole intellectual life arising out of it. This implies, of course, that it is in some way possible, if only as a loving gift originating from this Center, for me to achieve actual union with this ultimate Fullness, the ultimate *Whereunto* of my whole intellectual life.

At this point the objection naturally arises—and it deserves the most careful consideration and personal reflection to test out its validity concretely in our inner life—why there could not be a *third* alternative. Why could it not be that the human mind would be adequately fulfilled and entirely content as long as it was assured of inexhaustible novelty, an unending series of finites to know and enjoy? I am well aware that such an alternative may seem plausible at first blush, but working through it carefully in a thought experiment will, I think, show clearly enough that it must finally collapse. Such an alternative must be set in a framework of immortality and eternity of time; otherwise the series would come to an end without fulfillment: fulfillment depends necessarily in this conception on the *unending* sequence. In this perspective, surely a series of endless repetitions of the same *kind* of finite satisfactions, a mere quantitative repetition, would eventually pall and leave us open again to a profound and insatiable restlessness. For the human mind—and will—has a remarkable and wonderful capacity to transcend whole series at a time, to sum up their quality if not their quantity; and if the former remains always finite, the mind at once leaps beyond the whole series questing for a qualitative *more*, a *richer* final goal.

This at once launches us in a new direction, no longer along merely horizontal lines at the same level of things, but in a vertical ascent toward qualitatively ever-higher and richer realities. Once we have moved into the spiritual realm here, we would be into immortal entities, and an *actually* infinite number of them. If there are causal links of any kind between the degrees of being, as is likely, it is not clear that such a structure makes sense. But even if it did, the mind could comprehend this whole ascending series, its appetite expanding as it rises, and long to leap ahead to the really greatest and best—or at least one much further advanced—and not have to wait for unending eternity and never actually get there. With no *possibility* of ever reaching the best, the infinite series would again evoke a profound frustration at this eternal unfulfillableness.

To sum up, we have not really taken full possession of our own inner dynamism of inquiry until we keep penetrating to its profoundest depths and suddenly become aware in a kind of epiphany of self-discovery precisely that its very nature is to be an inexhaustible abyss that can comprehend and leap beyond any finite or series of finites, unending or not. This involves perhaps more existential self-discovery than logical or abstract reasoning.

My final point is that the notion of an Infinite Plenitude and union with it leads many people to a certain block, because this is conceived as a static state—finished once and for all with nothing further going on. But there is no reason to conceive of the infinite and total fulfillment through union with it in this way. It is more natural to think of it as a fullness out of which continually and spontaneously overflow free creative *expressions* of ecstatic joy. These are not *necessary steps on the way* to achieve fulfillment, but a natural, spontaneous overflow of *expression* because we *have reached* it. There would still be endless novelty, but no longer as fulfilling ever-insatiable *need*.

Now that we have again reduced our ultimate alternatives to two, the crucial question arises: which of these two is actually the case? Which should I opt for? Which is the more reasonable to opt for? On the one hand is the acceptance of myself, in the profoundest depths of my intellectual nature, as a living frustration, an existential absurdity, ordered ineluctably toward a simply non-existent goal, magnetized, so to speak, by the abyss of nothingness, of what is not and can never be—a dynamism doomed eternally to temporary gratification but permanent unfulfillment. On the other hand lies the acceptance of my nature as drawn, magnetized toward an actually existing, totally fulfilling goal, which confers upon it total and magnificent meaningfulness and opens out before it a destiny filled with inexhaustible light and hope. On the one hand, the darkness of ultimate nothingness of what can never be; on the other, the fullness of ultimate Light, which already awaits our coming.

How is this most radical of all options to be decided? The founder of Transcendental Thomism, Joseph Maréchal—and perhaps most others in this tradition—insist that the structure of human thought as oriented toward Infinite Being is a necessary *a priori* structure or condition of possibility of all our thinking. We cannot help, if we think at all, living in the limitless horizon of being and tending toward the fullness of being as fulfilling goal; we cannot help but make all our judgments by affirming every finite being against the implicit background of the infinite, as stepping-stones toward the infinite. "Man is an embodied affirmation of the Infinite," as Father Donceel likes to put it. We can conceptually and verbally deny the existence of this Infinite as the ultimate

Whereunto of our whole drive to know. But the very exercise of the mind even in the most ordinary everyday affirmation implicitly reaffirms what we explicitly deny, putting us not in a logical but in a lived contradiction with ourselves. We are committed *a priori*, by nature, to the affirmation of the reality of the infinite—whether we call it by the term "being" or some other, or only point to it in eloquent silence—no matter how much we deny it on the conscious, explicit level of our knowing.

There is much to be said for this strong position. However, I myself prefer to dig a little deeper, if possible, and move the option into the realm of a radical existential decision in the order of freedom, of free self-assumption of our own nature as gift. For it does seem that the above argument for the rigorous necessity of this implicit affirmation of God in all knowing rests on the tacit assumption that the dynamism of my intelligence does actually make ultimate sense, is not a radical absurdity, and hence must have some really existing final goal, since an existing dynamism without goal would be unintelligible. Yet modern man—as Sartre, Camus, and others have shown—does seem to have an astonishing capacity for self-negation as well as self-affirmation, irrational as this may be. Man is the being who can affirm or deny his own rationality.

Hence it seems to me that there is no *logical argument* by which one can be *forced* to choose one side of the option, light or darkness, rather than the other. The issue lies beyond the level of rational or logical argument because it is at the root of all rationality. Hence I would like to propose it as a radical option open to man's freedom: he is free to assume his own rational nature as gift and follow its natural call to total fulfillment, or else to reject this call and refuse to commit himself, on the level of conscious affirmation and deliberately lived belief, to the summons of his nature calling from the depths of the dynamism of intelligence as such. All the light lies on one side, and our whole nature positively pulls us in this direction; only ultimate darkness lies on the other, and cannot pull us as either rational or good. But we do remain free, I am willing to allow, to make this radical assumption, to accept our own nature, or to reject it. This existential choice, obscure and implicit though it may be (and though it may never reach the conceptual clarity and explicitness of a choice for "God" or "no God"), is still the most important choice of our lives, giving ultimate form and meaning to the whole.

If I accept and listen to this radical innate pull of my nature as intellectual being, if I accept this nature gratefully and humbly as a gift, I will affirm with conviction the existence of the ultimate Fullness and Center of all being, the lodestar that draws my intelligence ever onward, even though this ultimate goal remains for me at present only obscurely discerned, seen through a mirror darkly, pointed to beyond all conceptual grasp as the mystery of inexhaustible Light, a Light that with my present, body-obscured vision I cannot directly penetrate or master with my own powers, but that renders all else intelligible.

The Ascent through the Dynamism of the Will

The same process of discovery works even more powerfully and effectively—from the point of view of its psychological impact—when applied to the correlative dynamism of the human will, operating within the limitless horizon of being as the good, as the valuable and lovable.[8] Reflecting on the operation of my human will, I come to discover or unveil the nature of this faculty, or active potency in Thomistic terms, as an unrestricted and inexhaustible drive toward the good, as presented by my intelligence. Our entire life of willing, desiring, loving, avoiding, is carried on within the horizon of the good, the formal object of the will as such. But this horizon of being as the good, like that of being as truth for the intellect, reveals itself to be also unlimited, unbounded. The process of discovery is similar. Each time we take possession of some new finite good, we are temporarily satisfied as we explore and enjoy its goodness for us. But again, as soon as we discover its limits, its finitude, our wills at once spontaneously rebound beyond, in prospective desire and longing for further fulfillment. Over and over throughout our lives this process is repeated.

Reflecting now on this process as a whole, we can disengage its meaning in the light of its final cause or goal. Its ultimate goal, through which alone this dynamism—like any dynamism—is rendered intelligible, can be nothing less than the totality of the good, whatever that may turn out to be. There is, therefore, in the will a dynamic *a priori* orientation toward the good as such—i.e., a natural affinity, connaturality, aptitude for the good—which is written into the very nature of the will as dynamic faculty before any particular experience of an individual good, and defines this nature as such. Everything it desires and loves it loves *as good*, as situated within this all-embracing horizon of the good, as participating in some way in the transcendental character of goodness.

Now this *a priori* orientation and natural affinity for the good implies that the will, in order to recognize and respond to a good when it finds it, must have written within it—analogously to the intellect—a pre-conceptual "background consciousness," an anticipatory grasp—unthematized or implicit, obscure and indistinct—of the good as somehow present in its very depths, magnetizing and attracting it, luring it on to actual fulfillment of its innate potentiality by distinct conscious appropriations of actually existing concrete goods. This is what it means to live volitively in the horizon of the good. The entire life of the will consists in filling in determinately and concretely this unbounded, all-embracing, indeterminate, intentional horizon of the good as anticipated field of all possible fulfillment. As Plato said long ago in the *Meno*, in one of his profoundest insights, in any inquiry or search, unless we somehow dimly and implicitly knew ahead of time what we were looking for, we would never recognize an answer as an answer to our search. The passage is not from total non-knowledge or absence of the good to knowledge or presence, but from implicit and indistinct to explicit and distinct awareness. As St. Thomas put it in a striking formula, often highlighted by Transcendental Thomists, "Every knower knows God implicitly in anything it knows."[9] Similarly, every will implicitly loves God in anything it loves.

We must now analyze more precisely what must be the content of this unlimited horizon of the good, ever-present by anticipation as implicit "background consciousness" in the will and drawing it like a lodestar or hidden magnet. This analysis can be set, if one wishes, in the outer form of an Aristotelian demonstration; but in fact its inner soul is the drawing out into explicitness of what is already necessarily contained implicitly in the life of the will, if the latter is not to collapse into unintelligibility. The horizon of the good appears to us first as a vague, indefinite, indeterminate totality. It must be somehow a unity, first because of the analogous similarity of all that draws the will *as good*, second because the unity of any dynamism or active potency is at least partly dependent on the unity of its goal. A totally unrelated multiplicity of final goals would fragment the unity of the dynamism into an unintelligible, unintegrated multiplicity of drives. Now as we analyze the dynamism of the will, as above, we discover that no finite particular good can be its adequate final goal for it at once rebounds beyond any finite object once its limits have been discovered. And just as no one finite can satisfy adequately this drive, neither can any sum of all finite members, not even an endless series of all finite goods. Once the mind has gathered, in a single synthetic act of comprehension, the meaning of the whole series, and realizes that this is all there ever will be, or can be, it then becomes clear that the will would be doomed to an unfillable, insatiable abyss of longing—in a word, an ultimate frustration, an ontological surd. It would be an actually existing dynamism, ordered by an *a priori* orientation constitutive of its very nature—about which, therefore, it can do nothing—ordered precisely toward a non-existent final goal; an active potency ordered toward nothing proportionate to its potentiality; an innate drive toward nothing.

The only other alternative is that within this limitless, indeterminate horizon of the good lies hidden as its center and source an actually existing Infinite Plenitude of Goodness—not this or that particular good, but the Good itself, subsisting in all its essential unparticipated fullness—from which all finite goods possess their limited goodness by participation. In this case the dynamism of the human will takes on ultimate and magnificent sense, is ordered toward a totally fulfilling final goal which must be at least possible for it to obtain (whether by its own power or by free gift is not yet clear), and the whole of human life takes on the structure of hope rather than of frustration and absurdity.

Again, as in the case of the drive of the intellect toward being as truth, we are brought up against a radical option. To which alternative shall we—ought we—commit ourselves? Again, some of the Transcendental Thomists say that whether we like it or not we are committed by the dynamism of final causality built into our nature to affirm implicitly the *actual existence* of the Infinite Good, since if it were only possible, no finite being could make it actual. If we deny it on the conscious conceptual and verbal level, as we are free to do, we put ourselves in a state of lived—not logical—contradiction between the actual use of our power of willing and what we say about it. As St. Thomas would say, all lovers implicitly love God in each thing they love.[10]

But again, as I proposed above in the case of the intellect, this stand, impressive and defensible though it may be, still seems to me to presuppose as already accepted the intelligibility of the life of the will, and modern man has the ability to put the very intelligibility of his own nature radically in question. Hence I prefer again to propose the option as appealing to the radical freedom of each human person to assume or reject, freely, the ultimate meaningfulness of his or her own human nature as power of willing and loving the good. No *logical* argument can force me to choose one alternative over the other. Yet the luminous fullness of meaningfulness draws me with the whole spontaneous pull of my nature toward the real existence of the Infinite Good as a magnet fully adequate to, even far exceeding, the profoundest imaginable reaches of my capacity for love. Full intelligibility lies only this way. On the other side, there is only the prospect of an endless chain of unfinished and interminable business, trailing off into the darkness of ultimate frustration—an abyss to whose profoundest longing cry there can be no responsive echo. If I humbly and gratefully accept my nature with its natural pull toward the Infinite as a meaningful gift, I will commit myself to affirm—and to reach out with anticipatory, hope-filled love toward—a Center of Infinite Goodness as actually existing and somehow possible for me to be united with, though veiled from me at present in mystery.

This approach to God through the dynamism of the will toward the good has a far more powerful appeal to most people than the approach through the intellect alone as ordered toward truth. Many people, at least in certain moods and at certain times of their lives, feel that they could do without the fullness of knowledge; at least its drawing power is not overwhelming. But there is nobody, intellectual or not, who is not constantly and wholeheartedly longing for happiness. This is the deepest and most urgent of all drives in man—in fact, the dynamo behind all others. For as St. Thomas points out, unless possessing the truth appeared to us as a good attracting the will, we would not be drawn to seek knowledge at all.

I would like to share with you, as an example, a case from my own experience. One day I was in a cab in New York City. The cab driver being very talkative, I decided to turn the conversation to some useful purpose. So I asked him if he was happy. "No, too many problems," he answered. "What would make you happy then?" I asked. "Give me a million dollars and all my problems would be solved. I'd be a happy man and could enjoy life." "All right," I replied, "you have the million dollars. Now what?" Then he said he would pay off all his debts. "All right, they are paid. Now what?" Then he said he would buy a house. Several, in fact. "Done," I replied. "Now what?" Then he got himself a nice wife—in fact several, in different cities. "Done. Now what?" Then he traveled, went through a whole long set of things he wanted to do; and each time I replied the same: "Granted. Now what?" Finally he began to quiet down. Then he suddenly turned all the way around, in the middle of traffic, giving me quite a scare, and said: "Say, something funny is going on here. I can't seem to get to the bottom of all this. What am I really looking for after all?" He had suddenly totaled up the whole series, past *and to come*, and caught the point. Then I began . . .

Response to Tillich

Let us return now to Tillich's criticism, with which we began our exposition. It should be clear, I think, that this inner way of the mind to God, first developed formally and explicitly by the Transcendental Thomists within the Thomist tradition as an argument or rational vindication for the affirmation of the existence of God, is quite different from the Aristotelian-type argument to God through cosmic motion, which Tillich found fault with for beginning with God as absent and proceeding to search for Him somewhere outside us. The inner ascent to God through the dynamism of the human spirit starts rather with a God who is actually *present* from the beginning in the depths of our knowing and willing activities, because He is actually and efficaciously drawing us all the time toward Himself. But this presence is at first only implicit, veiled, dimly and obscurely intuited—perhaps "felt" would be better—in our pre-conceptual awareness of the un-limited horizons of being and goodness. The process of bringing this implicit, lived awareness into explicit, reflectively self-conscious and rationally grounded affirmation may take a long time and much intellectual discussion and groping. It may even take the form of a chain of Aristotelian syllogisms, though I, myself, do not think this method is appropriate to the subject matter. But it is still not the search for a God who is ontologically or even psychologically—in the deep sense—absent. It is the unveiling, the uncovering *within us* of the God who has always been there, existentially drawing us to Himself, but not yet recognized as such. A journey is indeed needed to find a God who *appears* to be absent at first in the order of explicit conceptual knowledge. But it is a journey within, into the depths of my own self, to discover the treasure always present there but hidden at first from the clouded vision of my sense-bound eyes.

By this turn to the inner way the contemporary Transcendental Thomists, stimulated by the challenge of Kantian agnosticism to a realistic epistemology, metaphysics, and philosophy of God, have brought to light a hitherto largely undeveloped dimension of the authentic thought of St. Thomas. In so doing they have significantly corrected and enriched the apparent one-sidedness of the exclusively cosmic and "exterior" approach to God characteristic of the original Thomistic Five Ways and their traditional elaboration in the classical Thomist school. And in so doing, these contemporary Thomists have also, through the unlikely intermediary of Kant, rejoined in their own way the ancient Platonic path through the *eros* of the soul, which gives it wings to ascend to Absolute Unity, Goodness, and Beauty—a path which was so creatively assimilated into Christian thought in the West by the Augustinian tradition and worked so powerfully within it for a thousand years before St. Thomas and the rise of Aristotelian-inspired scholasticism.

Dynamism of the Spirit as the Image of God in Man

Before leaving this topic, we should not fail to note that this Thomistic analysis of the dynamism of the spirit also provides us with a profound metaphysical analysis of the ancient religious-mystical-philosophical doctrine of man as the image of God, principally through the intellect and will. For man to be truly the image of God in any strong sense, it would seem appropriate (necessary?) that there be some mark or manifestation of the divine infinity itself in man. This obviously cannot be a positive infinite plenitude; that is proper to God alone. But there can be an image of the divine infinity in silhouette—in reverse, so to speak—within man, precisely in his possession of an *infinite capacity* for God, or, more accurately, a capacity for *the Infinite*, which can be satisfied by nothing less. This negative image points unerringly toward the positive infinity of its original, and is intrinsically constituted by this relation of tendential capacity. It is as though—as with the ancient myths—God had broken the coin of His infinity in two, holding on to the positive side Himself and giving us the negative side, then launching us into the world of finites with the mission to search until we have matched our half-coin with His. By this only we shall know that we have reached the goal of our lives, our final happiness.[11]

In connection with this notion of the dynamism of the spirit as a veiled revelation of ourselves as image of God, I share with you an interesting experiment I have tried with marked success on many student groups and individual people. It is an attempt to answer the common complaint one so often hears: Why is it that God remains so obscure and difficult to find? With His omnipotent power, you would think it would be the easiest thing in the world for Him to reveal Himself with perfect clarity to almost anybody, without having to pass through the obscurity of faith or the difficulty of philosophical argument.

My answer is this. All right, suppose you are God, omniscient and omnipotent. Now suppose you wanted to manifest your true nature to men, as *Infinite Spirit*. You can use any means—but not faith, or direct mystical experience, because most people are not prepared for that and could not receive it or interpret it properly; it takes a long process of purification to be able to receive it without distortion. You think it would be such an easy job—if you were God. Go ahead and try. What would you do?

Some come up with sensational physical cures. I laugh, and point out that some higher spaceman could do that. Others would produce great natural cataclysms, whirling planets, and so forth. I point out that these things do presuppose a much higher power than ours, but not an *infinite* power, let alone a pure spirit. I keep on knocking down every physical or psychic feat they produce as nowhere near the mark. When they have finally given up, I suggest that maybe it's not such an easy thing to do after all, even for God. Maybe God, too, has His own problems with self-manifestation to man. Then I suggest that there may perhaps be only one way even for God to do this: by leaving some mark of His infinity imprinted within us. But the only kind possible is a negative infinity of capacity and longing, which can only be matched by His own self, and hence, even though it gives us no positive clear picture of Him, nevertheless serves us as a guide to eliminate all other contenders less than Himself for our final goal. Thus this apparently obscure way of revealing Himself may in fact be the best if not the only one available, given our situation and His. If we explore it all the way to its depths, our dynamism for the infinite turns out to be a remarkably eloquent reverse image and pointer toward God as He is in Himself, beyond all possible finites.

Comparison with Augustinian Tradition

Yet the significant philosophical differences between the Augustinian and the Thomistic traditions remain within this common inner path. One difference, for example, is that Augustinians like St. Bonaventure tend to give the impression—in fact, assert quite explicitly—that God as Infinite Being is somehow present to the mind of man as a kind of uncreated Light, through whose light we then come to know all eternal truths, eternal value judgments, and finite beings as finite. Through the light of Being we know all beings, just as through the Good we love all goods. The *ontological* order of the priority of God as First Cause and our radical dependence on Him for all knowing and loving tends to be identi-

fied here with the *epistemological and psychological* order of our
discovery of God (though some are inclined to think this
may be due more to technical imprecision of concepts and
methodology than to irreconcilable doctrinal differences).[12]
Another significant difference—due to more than technical
imprecision, I think—derives from their differing analyses of
the cognitive process in man, specifically the relation of intellect to sense, rooted in the relation of soul to body. For the
medieval Augustinian tradition, the soul had two "faces."
One, the Aristotelian face, looked downward toward the
material world, known through sensory knowledge, from
which the intellect abstracted the essences of material things
in the mode of Aristotelian abstraction. But there was another face of the soul, its Platonic or spiritual face, which
looked directly and intuitively into the realm of spiritual
being—including its own soul as spiritual, other spirits
(angels), and God Himself, the Supreme Spirit—without
passing through the mediation of sense knowledge and the
abstraction of intelligible forms from it.[13] For St. Thomas,
on the other hand, there was no such independent upper face
of the soul which could look directly on its own into the
higher spiritual world, without at least the initial mediation
of the sense world. Because of the intrinsic interdependent
unity of soul and body—hence of intellect and sense—in
man, all his *natural* knowledge was intrinsically sensitive-intel-
lectual in origin, though the act itself of intellectual insight
and its final products, concept, and judgment transcend the
body and its senses.[14] St. Thomas makes an explicit exception, of course, for *supernatural* mystical knowledge of God,
which he held was directly infused by God at the so-called

fine point of the spiritual soul, bypassing all its faculties, both sensitive and rational. (One has the impression that the Augustinian tradition never clearly distinguished the natural from the mystical or supernatural modes of human knowing, and that this accounts at least partly for their expressed differences from the Thomistic tradition.)

As a result of this close union of intellect and sense in St. Thomas, man could come to the knowledge of himself as spirit and of the higher spiritual world only by first awakening his intellect through understanding the material world and his relation to it, then—"led by the hand" by material things, as St. Thomas colorfully puts it—ascend to God as the ultimate Source both of the world and of himself.[15] This does not mean that man cannot rise to God through the inner path of his own soul, but that when he does, the *élan* of his mind must always lean on some sensible image or symbol as a springboard to take off from. It means also that our natural knowledge of God in this life can never attain to a pure, direct spiritual intuition or clear conceptual representation of His nature, but can only point to Him through very general open-ended analogous concepts as that which is required by the mind's radical exigency for intelligibility: affirmed as the ultimate Source of all being, intelligibility, and goodness, but at present wrapped in mystery for the cloudy finite vision of our embodied minds, unable to gaze directly on the Infinite Light. Thus for St. Thomas—and for the Transcendental Thomists, faithfully following him on this point—the content of our natural knowledge of God, known through the dynamism of the human spirit as the ultimate fulfilling *Whereunto* of its exigency for the fullness of

being as truth and goodness, is considerably more indirect
and modest than that of Augustinian man. And, as we shall
see in Part II of this book, this inner path of discovery of
God through the transcendental analysis of the *a priori* conditions of possibility of the dynamism of the human spirit as
knower and lover needs to be completed by the so-called
outer path of cosmic ascent to God, by which we reach God
not just through final causality—*as* my God, my ultimate
satisfaction—but through efficient causality also as God the
Creator, the ultimate Source of all being and goodness in the
universe.

St. Thomas also diverges from St. Augustine and the Augustinian tradition in another significant way. Augustine in
his *De Libero Arbitrio* lays out his famous argument for the
existence of God from the existence of eternal truths, which
are "given" but require the existence of an eternal mind, i.e.,
God, thinking them as their foundation. Without mention-
ing Augustine, St. Thomas quietly undermines the possibility
of any such Platonic-based argument by pointing out that
since truth resides only in an intellect, there are no eternal
truths given us unless they are already thought by an eternal
intellect, i.e., God (*Summa Theologiae*, I, q. 16, art. 7).

Conclusion

Despite these reservations, the development by contemporary
Transcendental Thomists of an authentically Thomistic
inner way to the philosophical discovery of God is a major
new contribution to and enrichment of the 700-year-old
Thomistic tradition. It seems to me also that it responds

much more adequately and sensitively to the demands of contemporary religious thinkers in the existentialist-personalist tradition, like Tillich himself, for whom the feeling for the radical difference between the human person—with its inner life of self-consciousness, freedom, and love—and the non-personal material cosmos is so acute that if God is not found as immanent within the human person, He cannot be found at all. I myself believe, with St. Thomas, that the truly Christian God must be found as immanent both within the person and within the cosmos, as Lord of both the inner and the outer world. But that is the subject of our next section.

The Metaphysical Ascent to God through Participation and the Analogical Structure of Our Language about God

In the book's first section we presented the new turn to the inner path of philosophical ascent to God, through the dynamism of the human spirit and its *a priori* conditions of intelligibility, as developed by contemporary Transcendental Thomists. We showed how it corrected a too-extraverted, exclusively cosmological approach to God which had been characteristic of traditional Thomistic natural theology. However, taken by itself, this inner path is one-sided and incomplete. It must be paired, it seems to me, with a more cosmically oriented metaphysical approach if we are to reach the full notion of God. This section will develop this second approach to see how it enables us to speak meaningfully about God through an analogical structure of thought and language.

Why the Inner Path Is Insufficient

Why is the inner path to God through the dynamism of the human spirit insufficient by itself to deliver the full content of the traditional notion of God?

If taken strictly by itself, as proceeding in the order of final causality alone, this approach does deliver, I think, eminently reasonable grounds for affirming the existence of an infinitely perfect *being* as my God, my ultimate fulfillment of both intellect and will. But this conclusion does not of itself give me the warrant to assert this same God as the ultimate *source* of all being, including my own. In a word, it does not deliver the knowledge of God as *Creator of all things*. To know God as *Omega*, as goal, is not *ipso facto* to know Him as *Alpha*, as source. It is indeed plausible to suppose that, once we have discovered the existence of an infinite being as our goal, it will also turn out to be the Source of all finite beings. Still, the argument from final causality by itself does not deliver this conclusion explicitly. Yet without this conclusion we do not yet know the true God in His full meaning: as *at once* my God and God of the cosmos. The God of authentic religion must always be both, the God of *Genesis* as well as *Exodos*. To reach this fuller conclusion I must make a new start. I must turn to the rest of the vast universe of beings outside myself and raise the question for them as to what they need to fulfill the exigencies of intelligibility respecting their own actual existence. I have seen that God is needed to make ultimate sense out of my life as the ultimate goal of its dynamic tendency. Is He needed to make ultimate sense for me *out of* their being as well, as the very source of their being, and of mine too? The questions, though closely connected, are not identical. Nor can they be answered by the same argument. This point is sometimes forgotten by enthusiasts for the inner path, including by some Transcendental Thomists. The inner path and the cosmic path are sisters who must walk hand in hand if they are to reach their common goal of the true God. What we need to do, then, is to raise the question of the intelligibility of the whole realm of the beings of my experience, and then of all finite beings. The answer to this question cannot be found in the dynamism of my own spirit considered in itself alone, but in the wider reach of the metaphysics of being itself. Or, if you wish, it will be found in the application of the dynamism of my intelligence to the quest for the intelligibility of *all* being.

To be fair to those Transcendental Thomists who prefer to combine the two approaches in a single argument from the dynamism of the spirit, as does Father Donceel in his

Natural Theology, I think it is possible to develop the argument in such a way that it would include both thrusts of the mind as complementary movements toward the fullness of intelligibility. For the same act of rebounding of the mind beyond any and all finites can be unfolded under two aspects: one is the necessary movement toward the Infinite as the search for the fulfillment of *my own* dynamism as such, quite independent of this particular finite being I am rebounding beyond; the other is the necessary movement of the mind toward the Infinite as searching for the full intelligibility of this very finite *being itself* I have just laid hold of and am trying to understand. The two are indeed closely intertwined, and perhaps only abstractly separable. However, the two modalities of explanation through final cause or goal and through efficient cause or origin still seem to me so distinct in the reasons grounding them that it is a little confusing to fuse them into a single argument without leaving too much implicit. Hence I prefer to follow out the two lines separately, partly for the sake of clarity, partly to maintain my links with the long and explicit tradition of analysis through efficient causality that is so deeply ingrained in St. Thomas himself and has always been one of the chief bonds of union between all Thomistic schools.

Deficiencies of St. Thomas's "Five Ways"

Does this mean that I am going to treat you, willy-nilly, to an exposition of the famous classical Five Ways of St. Thomas?[1] Not at all. First of all, I consider them in their actual textual form to require too much adaptation to convince the ordinary modern thinker. Second, I do not think that they represent the best of St. Thomas's own truly original and most characteristic metaphysical structure of ascent to God as shown in the rest of his works.

The main trouble with the Five Ways is that they are too incomplete as they stand. There are other troubles too, as we shall see. The first three are Aristotelian and for that very reason incomplete. The first two—from motion or change and from chains of efficient causality—conclude only to a Prime Mover, a First Cause, in the particular causal series which each is posited to explain. They do not and cannot deliver a single, infinitely perfect Source of all being. The same difficulty is found in the Fifth Way, from order in the world (though this is not of Aristotelian origin). It reaches a Cosmic Planner—or possibly Planners, since the argument by itself does not establish whether this Planner is one or many, nor whether it is the Planner only for our material cosmos or for all existing and possible universes. Still, this argument, if properly filled out, remains a very effective first major step toward establishing the existence of God, and has always been a popular way in traditions of thought both Eastern and Western—so popular that St. Thomas calls it the "most efficacious way" for people generally in all times and cultures.[2] But as it stands it is extremely condensed and incomplete.

The Third Way, from contingent beings (which means for St. Thomas corporeal beings which come into being and pass away) is an extremely difficult and controversial one in its internal formal structure.[3] Despite desperate attempts by many Thomists to save it, it seems to me not merely incom-

plete but formally invalid in its logical form because it necessarily depends for its efficacy on an unexpressed
principle—namely, that given infinite time, all possibilities
will come true. One such possibility is that all contingent
beings together should at some time have ceased to be. Since
that possibility must have already come true, given infinite
past time, *then* if all beings in the universe were contingent,
nothing at all would now exist: out of nothing no-thing at
all could ever come. Hence there must exist at least one necessary being. The argument proceeds soundly from this point
on, save that it does not conclude to a single infinite Source
of all being. But the key principle at work in the first part of
the argument—that all possibilities must come true, given
infinite time—seems to me not only not provable but actually not true at all. For another equally plausible state of
affairs is that each corruptible being should generate another
before it perished, and so on forever; the two logical possibilities, like many such cases, are not co-possible in the same
universe.

It is rare that St. Thomas falls into any genuine logical or
epistemological slips. But I think, with many others, that he
has fallen into a serious one here, following precisely the lead
of his master Aristotle, who asserts and tries to prove in *De
Caelo* (book 1, chapters 11–12) that if a body did not actually
"corrupt" (i.e., perish), given infinite time, then it would be
incorruptible, could not perish—that every real potency must
be fulfilled, given infinite time. His argument is intriguing,
but quite invalid, it seems to me. The whole argument is a
complex and fascinating one, which we have no time to go
into here, but it is strewn with so many logical and meta-

physical booby traps that it hardly provides a solid and effective basis for affirming the existence of God, even in Aristotle's and St. Thomas's time, let alone our own. Most Thomistic manuals—and even a few distinguished commentators like the great Gilson himself—discreetly (but none too honestly, to my mind) sidestep the whole problem by substituting (for purposes of simplicity and brevity, as they put it) the apparently similar but much briefer argument from the *Summa contra Gentes* (book 1, chapter 15, 5; Pegis translation). This argument, quite a valid metaphysical one in its own right, proceeds on an entirely different principle requiring no recourse at all to the principle that all possibilities must come true, given infinite time.

The Fourth Way, the closest to St. Thomas's own personal Neoplatonically inspired metaphysics of participation, can be fixed up fairly easily to fit the latter. But as the argument is actually expressed in the text, appealing to a misreading of a terse text of the early Platonic period of Aristotle—a misreading apparently widely current in St. Thomas's time—the arrangement of premises follows an inverted and defective order. Beginning from degrees of perfection in the world, it concludes directly to a maximum as norm for ranking the other degrees, and then in a second moment tries to show that this maximum—which, so far as the force of the argument goes, might be a merely ideal norm—is also the efficient cause of all the limited degrees of perfection. This is an order, strange to say, that St. Thomas never follows elsewhere in his own metaphysics of participation and ascent from the finite to the Infinite, where he always passes across the bridge of efficient causality first in order to reach a real maximum. The reverse order, as found in the text of the argument, I consider to be of highly dubious metaphysical vintage and value, despite various attempts of Thomists to salvage it by appealing to exemplary causality. There is no valid passage in St. Thomas to exemplary causality except through the prior establishment of an efficient cause, in which the exemplary ideas reside. The text of Aristotle which St. Thomas quotes as authority is a mistranslation, widely quoted in the thirteenth century but later corrected by William of Moerbeke's translation and all modern translations. The text here used by Thomas runs: "Highest in a genus is the cause of all in the genus." The correct translation runs: "The cause of all in the genus is the highest in the genus." The inversion in the Greek is merely for rhetorical emphasis.[4]

These are some of the reasons why many contemporary Thomists today—especially Transcendental Thomists like Rahner and Lonergan—stay away from the Five Ways in developing their own presentation of Thomistic natural theology. This is definitely my position. I look on the Five Ways as quick, condensed sketches of philosophical approaches to God, laid down by St. Thomas at the beginning of his *Summa Theologiae*—intended for "beginners," by the way, as he tells us—deliberately not taken from his own personal participation metaphysics but drawn from the thought of pagan philosophers, especially the newly introduced Aristotle, *the* philosopher for Thomas and so many in his day, for the express purpose of showing that even the pagan philosophers could by the use of reason alone arrive at an initial knowledge of God. After this first step, St. Thomas comes in with his own more high-powered metaphysics, and later Revelation, to work out a full Christian, metaphysically guided theology of God. But these Ways as they stand are so condensed and incomplete—so tied in implicitly (the first three at least) to certain assumptions of the Aristotelian cosmological framework of the time, and as a result need so much explanation, qualification, revision, and supplementation to make sense to a modern reader—that the results are no longer worth the effort, save for scholarly historical purposes. I must warn you, however, that this view, which I have exposed to you quite candidly and forthrightly, is not shared by all Thomists today.

We can, however, first reconstruct from the Five Ways, beginning from the Second Way from efficient causality, a single synthetic argument that goes all the way to a single infinite Source of all being, as I have done in my *Explorations in Metaphysics* (chapter 8), and *The One and the Many: A Contemporary Thomistic Metaphysics* (chapter 14). Only the last part of the argument will be borrowed from the Thomistic participation metaphysics. I shall briefly restate this reconstruction of my own here.

THE COSMIC WAY

(1) All around us we see beings that lack their own sufficient reason for existing, and hence require an efficient cause. But every being in the universe cannot require an efficient cause. For then there would be an endless regress of causes with the necessary conditions for actual existence never fulfilled anywhere—which is unintelligible. Hence there must exist at least one self-sufficient, unconditioned being.

(2) But no self-sufficient being can be limited, finite, in its qualitative perfection. For then it would have to be the sufficient reason why it exists in this particular limited mode of perfection rather than another already existing or possible. But to do so it would have to pre-exist its own being and choose for itself this particular limited degree of perfection rather than another—which is impossible. Hence, since every finite being requires a cause for its existence, no self-sufficient being can be finite, but must be an infinite fullness of qualitative perfection.

(3) It immediately follows that there can only be one such infinite being. For if there were two such, at least one would have to lack something the other had and so would be finite, or simply fuse into identity with the other. Hence there must exist one single infinite Source of all being.

Ascent to God through Participation Metaphysics

As a result, what most contemporary Thomists who think this way and yet still wish to develop an authentic Thomistic metaphysical approach to God are actually doing today is drawing not from the primarily Aristotelian side of St. Thomas's thought, which the Five Ways express, but rather from the much richer and profounder resources of his Neoplatonically inspired participation metaphysics, the deepest and most original level of St. Thomas's metaphysics.[5] It is a personal synthesis which he constructed by (1) taking over the general formal structure of Neoplatonic participation theory, (2) emptying it of its excessive Platonic realism of ideas, (3) filling it with the new wine of his own quite original insight into the act of existence as the ultimate positive core of all real perfections—an act which is multiplied and diversified by reception into various limiting modes of essence, and (4) expressing the whole structure in a transformed Aristotelian terminology of act and potency. It is this existentialized participation metaphysics which will allow us, I hope to show, to ascend in only a few steps from any finite reality of our experience directly to God as unique, infinite Source of all reality, quite independent of any scientific assumptions from our own or any day. This same structure will also provide the ground for our ability to speak meaningfully about God in analogical language drawn from the perfections we find in creatures.

The rest of this lecture will be devoted to laying out in condensed form, first, this ascent to God through Thomistic participation metaphysics and, second, the analogical language built upon it. I must warn, however, that this ancient Neoplatonic ascent of the mind from the many to the One and from the finite to the Infinite is not the type of formal-logical argument that can (if indeed any argument for anything real can) force all minds to accept it with compelling logical rigor. Its power perhaps lies more in the evocation of a basic metaphysical insight which is then laid out in the form of an argument. It may be also that the efficacy of the arguments is so inextricably involved in a profound existential commitment of the living dynamism of the spirit to a truly personal quest for the full intelligibility of the universe that it can remain opaque if one stands back in a purely detached, abstract, logical perspective. The quest for the hidden Center of the universe, whose presence—or better, the exigency for whose presence—most of mankind seems to feel obscurely, dimly, and inarticulately in the ineffable recesses of their minds and hearts, may well have to be indissolubly a quest of the whole person, of the whole being of a man or woman. (This does not mean that I am quietly hedging my bets and opening an escape hatch to avoid rigorous critical reflection on the arguments.) With these preliminary cautions, let us put on our metaphysical wings.

First Argument: From the Many to the One

The first argument I propose is, in my opinion, the simplest, most streamlined, most direct of all metaphysical arguments for God that have ever been proposed. (I mean, of course, valid arguments, since, with just about all Thomists, I consider the famous Ontological Argument—i.e., from the very concept of God to His actual existence, which is indeed briefer—to be incorrigibly invalid.) The first argument moves in a single step from the beings of our experience, taken simply *as many* and *existing*, to *a single Infinite Source* of all being and all perfection. I love it myself, as I am sure St. Thomas did and Plotinus in his own way before him did, but it is not always easy to share this vision.

Let me first read one of St. Thomas's own succinct versions of it—which, I might add, I have a strong suspicion that most of you, even professional philosophers, have never heard proposed as a Thomistic proof for God. In fact, in the article in question—Question 3, Article 5 of his *Disputed Question on the Power of God (De Potentia)*—he is not formally seeking to prove the existence of God, but rather to establish that there can be only one *single* Creator of all things, that all things outside Him must be created by Him alone. In so doing he establishes in a single sweep of thought both *that* there is a creator and that there is *a single one* of all things. The text reads thus, in my translation:

> It is necessary that if some one attribute is found in common among many things, it be caused in them by some one cause. For it cannot be that this common attribute belongs to each one as derived from its own self (*ex se ipso*), since each one, according as it is its own unique self, is distinguished from every other, and a diversity of causes produces a diversity of effects. Therefore, since the act of existence (*esse*) is found common to all things (shared by all things), which, according to *what* they are, are distinct from each other, it must be that their act of existence is communicated to them not from their own selves but from some one cause. And this seems to be the reasoning of Plato, who maintained that before all multiplicity there is a unity, not only in numbers but in real things.

Similar arguments, with slight variations, are found elsewhere.[6] Let us paraphrase their common essence. Whenever a real common attribute or perfection is shared among many, its only adequate ontological grounding is a single common source (efficient cause) for all, which possesses this common perfection in all its fullness. The reason is that the *common sharing* of the same perfection—i.e., the *real similarity* between all the members in the order of this perfection—needs an adequate sufficient reason or ontological grounding, and it cannot be *because* these sharers are *many* and *diverse* that they have something in common, that they are really *similar*. For real similarity—though it is not identity—is still a mode of unity, and diversity and multiplicity as such cannot be the ground of any unity. Now if this common perfection as in each member had its *ultimate* origin or source totally from each individual member by itself as unique and individual, as self-sufficient and self-enclosed, then it would be their radical individual diversity and multiplicity which would be the cause for their similarity, for their common bond of community. This is not intelligible. Diversity as such can never be the cause of unity. Therefore, ontological similarity among many, to have an adequate sufficient reason, must be grounded somewhere in a *concrete ontological unity*, a single source from which all the others ultimately derive this common perfection by participation. This argument works indeed on the level of form/matter composite of the same species, the unifying factor being the *form* with its generative power. But the unity remains on the limited level of specific form only.

Now let us apply this general schema to the most basic and universally shared of all positive perfections, the act of existence itself. I say "act of existence" and not merely "existence," because for St. Thomas, actual existence is not merely a static state or minimum "fact"—i.e., the mere extrinsic referent of a true assertion—but an *intensive inner act of presence within* the thing itself which grounds the mental assertion about it: a kind of qualitative energy (*virtus essindi:* the power of *be-ing,* in St. Thomas's words), condensing within it all the positive perfection of anything real, "the act of all acts and the perfection of all perfections," as St. Thomas himself puts it in a famous phrase. "For no real perfection," he says, "can accrue to a man from his wisdom unless he actually is wise."[7] Now since existence is thus shared most really and universally by absolutely *all* beings, this radical bond of similarity and community between all that is must be explained, onto-logically grounded, by being traced back to some one ulti-mate common Source of existence for all beings—a Source which must not merely *have* existence in some limited way, but *be* the very subsistent fullness of existence itself, *Ipsum Esse Subsistens*, from which all others ultimately receive their own particular limited modes of being. And since existence is the most basic and all-inclusive of all positive perfections or attributes, outside which no being or perfection lies, save nothingness—and hence condenses into itself implicitly all positive perfections as diverse modes of active presence—in reaching one Source of all existence we have at a single stroke reached the unique, ultimate, hence infinite Source of all pos-sible perfections, a perfect description of what we mean by God, though not yet a fully explicated description. St. Thomas himself identifies this as the ancient Platonic path from the many to the One. It is applied by him not merely to participation in a world of ideas or forms but to participa-tion in the most radically concrete and existential of all per-fections, the power or energy of existence itself as the ultimate inner act of each real being.

This argument can be summed up extremely briefly, grasped in a single synoptic insight. Wherever there is a many sharing some real perfection, there must be a single common source for this perfection. Since existence itself is the most universally shared of all perfections, including all that is real in any way, there must be a single common ulti-mate Source of all existence from whence all others partici-pate in it, each in its own way. The same basic schema, of course, can be applied to other "pure perfections"—i.e., those containing no imperfection or limitation in their *meaning*—such as goodness, intelligence, power, love, unity, activity, etc.

This extremely condensed formulation of St. Thomas contains implicitly within it a few basic epistemological and metaphysical principles that must be made explicit for the argument to remain valid. The central one is the epistemological realism of Aquinas, which is needed as a critical corrective or qualification on the scope of application of the principle that wherever there is a many there must be a grounding one. For Plato, every universal idea automatically belonged to the realm of the "really real," so that for him the grounding idea behind the universal linguistic term *ipso facto* becomes a real causal grounding principle. For Thomas, with his Aristotelian realism, the vast majority of universal ideas drawn from our material cosmos are in fact only abstractions of intelligible forms from the individualizing matter or body in which alone they actually exist. Our knowledge of the act of existence, on the other hand, for Thomas, is not an abstraction from real existence—obviously—but rather the result of a judgment of actual existence. The application of the argument from the many to the one is valid, therefore, only for a few predicates like existence itself or some similar transcendental predicate like "good, active," etc. Here the one grounding the many shared instances must itself be in the order of actual existence.

For the full explication of the sharing (participation) relation also, the dialectic of finite and infinite is required. Hence we are immediately adding a second basic argument directly from any finite being to a single infinite source. This can also serve as an independent argument on its own.

Before we pass on to the next argument, I call attention to a significant characteristic of this one as related to the criticism by Paul Tillich of St. Thomas's approach to God that we mentioned in the first part of the book. If you recall, Tillich called St. Thomas the first Christian atheist because his Aristotelian proofs from motion to a Prime Mover seek to *demonstrate* or *prove* the existence of God—i.e., to start from God's *absence* in the initial data and then try to find Him elsewhere in the cosmos at the end of a chain of premises. The present type of Neoplatonically inspired participation argument from the many to the One, however—though it can indeed be laid out discursively in a series of premises like a syllogism, if one wishes—is really more in the nature of a synoptic insight into the *presence* of the One as reflected in the many. For the common shared perfection, though not identically the fontal One itself, is nonetheless the mark or sign, the reflected image, of the One *in* the many, since it transcends the self-enclosed diversity and otherness of each one of the many, uniting them in a common bond of shared perfection and thus *pointing implicitly* to the unifying Source that is at once beyond and yet imminent in them all. This argument does not move, like the Aristotelian proof through motion, from the absence of God in the changing being to His presence elsewhere, but rather from the already positive but imperfect mark of His concealed presence to His fully revealed presence. It is not a journey to find an absent one, save in the order of our cognitive awareness, but rather a coming to explicit recognition of what was already implicitly present under the veil of an imperfect image, similar to what we found in the inner path to God through the dynamism of the spirit as described in the book's first part.

It is one of the powerfully perennial attractions of the Neoplatonic style of philosophy that the inner spiritual ascent of the soul to the One and the outer metaphysical ascent through the cosmos reveal themselves as two sides of the same coin. The spiritual and the metaphysical are not closed off from each other, but mirror each other in different orders. Some of this reflected glow of the inner life of the spirit can be found in St. Thomas too, once we learn to live within his more austere and impersonal-sounding expositions of the metaphysical ascent to God through participation. The abstract metaphysical "reduction" (*reductio*: his favorite term for a metaphysical proof), which is a "drawing back" of the beings of our experience to their source through causal participation metaphysics, mirrors the existential inner journey of the soul home to God as its blissful fulfillment.[8] I might add, too, that this movement of the mind from the many to the One reflects what seems to be the most basic structure of the human mind's constant quest for intelligibility in all fields. To understand is ultimately to *unify*: it means first to discern the parts of anything clearly, but finally to unify them into a meaningful whole in itself and then with all else that we know. He who does not understand something as one, St. Thomas says, understands nothing.[9]

Second Argument: From the Finite to the Infinite

The second pathway of metaphysical ascent to God through participation is slightly more complex than the first. It involves a passage from the finite as finite to the Infinite, which is shown to be necessarily unique. It is thus a two-step argument. The first path above, moving directly from the many, as a many sharing a one, to the One as Source, did not even have to pass through the mediation of finitude or degrees of perfection. The present one does, but it has an added richness of its own in that it unveils the One explicitly as infinite. It is also one of the two great Neoplatonic paths of metaphysical ascent to God. I say Neoplatonic rather than Platonic here advisedly, because although Plato was the father of the ascent from the many to the One, he had not yet worked out the path from the finite to the Infinite. The reason is that, like all classical Greeks, including Aristotle, he still held that the finite was the perfect, the completed or finished-off typified by form, whereas the infinite was the imperfect, the unfinished and indeterminate, typified by the indeterminacy and incompleteness of formless matter by itself. Plato did, however, have an equivalent movement from the particular and imperfect to the absolute and perfect, the Good in itself, Beauty in itself, etc. But for him to have called the One and the Good "infinite" might well have seemed like a blasphemy, as though the most perfect were also the most incomplete and unfinished. Plotinus was the first to acknowledge explicitly a higher Infinite of perfection beyond the limits of form, in addition to a lower infinite of imperfection below form—i.e., in matter by itself. He was thus enabled to develop formally and explicitly the metaphysical ascent from the finite to the Infinite.

Now to the argument itself, after a brief prefatory note. The term "finite" which we shall be using here, always in connection with finite perfection, has nothing to do with a beginning or end in space and time, with a *quantitative* finite. It is a strictly *qualitative* notion, signifying a limited degree of an intensive perfection in the qualitative order, capable of higher and lower degrees of intensity. So, too, "infinite" does not mean having no end in space or time (although not a few ancient, medieval, and modern thinkers have been quite fuzzy on this, confusing metaphysical infinity of perfection with eternity or omnipresence). It means rather the unrestricted qualitative plenitude of a perfection as it is in its unparticipated state, contrasted with any limited mode of participation, which possesses the perfection in question imperfectly and incompletely.

The argument proceeds as follows:[10]

(1) Whenever we find a common perfection possessed by many beings in various finite or limited degrees, no finite possessor of this perfection can adequately explain its own being as this finite participant. The reason is this. Since many degrees are possible, there must be some reason why this participant has this perfection only in this limited degree and not in some other possible degree. But the finite possessor cannot explain its own finite possession as finite, for then, as self-explanatory, it would have to be itself the ultimate source of this perfection which it has only to a limited degree. But if it were the ultimate source of this perfection, there is no reason why it should not have it in all its possible fullness instead of imperfectly, partially. It does not make sense for the ultimate source of a perfection to have it only imperfectly, incompletely. Furthermore, even to possess it only partially it would have to determine its own nature to

participate only so much and no more. This would mean that it would already have to exist, prior to its own nature, in some indeterminate state, and then actively determine its own nature to be this particular limited mode of being. But it is evident that nothing can pre-exist its own nature, so to speak, and actively determine its own essence to be what it is, since it would first have to be an existing determinate nature in order to perform any action at all. All this makes no sense. Hence no finite possessor of a perfection can ever be the ultimate self-sufficient source of a perfection that it possesses only imperfectly and incompletely.

Every finite being, therefore, by the very fact that it is finite—i.e., possesses a given perfection in a limited degree—points beyond itself to an infinite Source which possesses the same perfection in all its unlimited fullness. Every finite is thus by its very nature a pointer toward the Infinite. It is an image, a road marker, that necessarily carries the dynamism of the mind beyond itself in a search for intelligibility that can end only with an actual Infinite, from which all finite degrees of participation ultimately proceed.

Now if we apply this general participation schema to the basic transcendental perfections which contain no imperfection or limit in their meaning and hence can be applied to God—such as existence, goodness, love, power, intelligence, etc.—of which the most fundamental for St. Thomas is existence itself, we find that every finite possessor of these perfections points beyond itself to an Infinite Plenitude-Source of the same, from which all finite possessors receive these perfections—primarily existence itself—according to the limited nature and capacity of each. There must, therefore, be an Infinite Source of existence itself, as the ground of all other perfections.

(2) Now *the second step* in the argument, from the Infinite to the One. This is an easy and quick one, generally admitted by all metaphysicians who are willing to deal with a qualitative metaphysical infinite at all. It is impossible for there to be two actually existing absolute infinities of perfection, for there could be nothing to distinguish them. All duality in being implies negation: A is not B. But all negation implies some limitation: one of the two must lack something that the other has; otherwise they would fuse into one. But then at least one of the two must be limited. Any positive qualitative infinity absorbs all other infinities of the same order of perfection into itself. And since we are dealing in the present case with the ultimate perfection of existence itself, an infinite in the order of existence must be the ultimate, most absolute infinity of all, excluding all others. We have reached, therefore, the unique, ultimate, infinite Source of all being, the ultimate mystery of Plenitude that is also the magnet and final goal of the entire dynamism of the human spirit, both intellect and will.

This argument is clearly not an Aristotelian one, for two reasons. First, because Aristotle's crucial decision to reject the whole Platonic doctrine of participation cut off all the paths by which he could ascend from this lower world to the divine except through motion. Second, like Plato himself, Aristotle still considered the finite to be the perfect and the infinite the imperfect, and thus could not posit the Supreme Being as infinite. However, as St. Thomas has adapted it from the various medieval Neoplatonic sources which transmitted it to him, he has first recast it in a more realistic and existential mode by applying it to participation in the basic perfection of existence itself as intensive qualitative act, then explained the derivation of the finite from the Infinite in terms of Aristotelian-inspired efficient and not merely exemplary causality, and finally reformulated the general participation schema in terms of a transformed act-potency composition structure also inspired by Aristotle—so that for St. Thomas (though not yet for Aristotle), act of itself was unlimited and could be limited only by reception into some limiting potency, forming various kinds of act-potency compositions.

This synthesis of Neoplatonic participation, Aristotelian act-potency and efficient causality, and his own notion of existence as intensive act and the core of all perfections, constitute the profoundly original and personal participation metaphysics of St. Thomas, which I consider as perhaps his greatest contribution to philosophical thought. This is his transposition into technical metaphysics of the ancient religious, mystical, and metaphysical vision of the world as image of God, imperfect and obscure though it may be, up whose degrees of participated perfection the soul can mount like a ladder, and then use them as springboard for its final metaphysical-mystical leap to the Infinite Fontal Source of the whole, hidden in mystery from our direct gaze but pointed to by every finite image, which necessarily bears the mark of its Source upon it, inscribed on its very nature as only finite.

This Neoplatonic dimension of St. Thomas's metaphysics was left somewhat in the shadow by his early disciples, even in the early phases of the Thomist revival of the late nine-teenth and early twentieth centuries. His Aristotelianism was traditionally stressed, against the ultra-realism of the Platonic tradition. Even Gilson never seemed quite willing to ac-knowledge the full extent and import of this dimension in St. Thomas, never quite going back on his early statement that St. Thomas had made a basic option for Aristotle and against Plato.[11] There is much truth in the above statement as to St. Thomas's epistemology and philosophy of man, but not as to his metaphysics. From about 1939 on, however, various researchers, working independently during the war, began to come out at the same time with impressive scholarly studies highlighting the central role of participation in St. Thomas's metaphysics.[12] Since that time, this Neoplatoni-cally inspired aspect of his thought has come more and more into central focus—although it is not entirely clear how much this has filtered down to the ordinary philosophical public which does not specialize in St. Thomas.

Three brief notations before we leave this argument. First, the argument, though laid out by me at some length in dis-cursive form, may well not be so much a formal-logical movement of the mind through several distinct and indepen-dent premises as a more direct reflective insight into the exi-gency for the Infinite in every finite, into the imperfectly imaged *presence* of the Infinite in every finite. Second, referring to Tillich's criticism discussed in this book's first part, we note that, as in the case of the inner path through the dyna-mism of the spirit, this metaphysical ascent through partici-pation has the character not so much of starting from the absence of God to find Him elsewhere as of progressively unveiling to our minds a presence that was always there, but concealed under the veil of an image. I venture to make the (I realize) highly controversial suggestion that all objective metaphysical arguments for the existence of God must eventually pass over one or both of these aforementioned paths, from the many to the One and from the finite to the Infinite, if they wish adequately to attain their end. For example, I myself think the perennial argument from dynamic order in the world to a transcendent planning Intelligence is a thoroughly sound and effective first step—one which actually may be enough for most people. But to get all the way to a single infinite Source of *all* being and *all* perfection, I believe that one must still make the last step across one of these two bridges, or something similar to them.

It would be wise, I think, in view of my audience, to stop here for a moment to add a postscript on the use of efficient causality in this argument.

(1) I am well aware that many post-Kantian philosophers of religion, including personalists such as Gabriel Marcel, Neo-Hegelians (following Hegel himself), and others, are convinced that the notion of efficient causality has become so restricted and impoverished by its use in science and in Humean-Kantian models of extrinsic antecedent-consequent sequences in time (on the model of Hume's famous billiard balls) that it is no longer fitted to express the far more profound and intimate relation of God to the world. Hence they prefer the language of "self-communication," or "self-expression," to express this relationship, rejecting the language of causality. I have no serious quarrel with this new "self-communication" terminology, as long as the expression

or communication is sufficiently other than the self expressing itself in them, so as to be somehow distinct in being, and
originates existentially from this self as source. This is an
enriched but almost exact equivalent of the Thomistic metaphysical causality. For St. Thomas, "every act is by its nature
self-communicative" through action, and every act of efficient causality is by its very nature a self-communication and
self-expression, at least in some minimal way. It is connatural
to all action to be a self-revelation of being. What terminology one uses is not crucial; it is the insight behind it that
counts. We would be willing to rephrase what we have developed in the previous pages and say that the world takes its
origin from God as His self-expression. The only difficulty
with using the language of self-expression in the context of
an ascent of the mind to discover the *existence* of God is the
obvious one that one can hardly speak of the world as the
self-expression of God until one has first discovered that
there *is* a Self of which the world is an expression. The causal
argument is not subject to such a circle.

(2) Another and much larger group of post-Kantian philosophers, again including many religious thinkers, is unwill-
ing to accept any use of efficient causality which moves from
something given in experience to some cause that lies beyond
the horizon of our human experience—at least of our *possible*
experience, as some qualify it. Thus many analytic philosophers, following Strawson and others,[13] are willing to do *descriptive* metaphysics—i.e., analysis of the most general
categories of our experience (reflected in our language, of
course), but ban all *explanatory* metaphysics—i.e., an analysis
which postulates the real existence of explanatory principles

(causes, etc.) beyond our experience. Anthony Quinton expresses it neatly when he says, "For a causal inference is only legitimate if it is at least possible to obtain evidence for the existence of the cause which is independent of the events it is said to explain."[14] Others allow explanatory causal chains as long as they move in a horizontal series linking one finite, empirically known being or event to another, but will allow no vertical causal chain moving from finite to Infinite, from empirical data to a transempirical, transcendent source.

To my mind, this is an entirely unjustified restriction of the traditional and much richer classical notion of cause and causal explanation found in almost all pre-Humean thought and still clearly dominant in our ordinary, everyday, practical life, including technology. The restricted notion, derived from Hume and Kant, presumes that we have built up our concept of causality from science, from the experience of regular law-governed sequences of antecedent and consequent events in nature or human activity, which we then link by a purely mental subjective law of psychological association (Hume) or an *a priori* categorical necessity (Kant), then name the "cause-effect relation." For Kant, as for Hume, such a relation can only be validly applied when *both* terms of the relation are found in experience and then linked together. It follows that such a causal relation can never be applied to the noumenal or real world outside the knower, not even within the knower to anything beyond the narrow circle of his empirical (sense-given) experience. There is no valid movement from within experience to anything outside it.

The older metaphysical and everyday concept of efficient cause and causal explanation is of quite different origin. The notion is first grasped indeed in the context of some sequence given in experience, such as moving our own body or moving other things with our body. But the *understanding of* the causal relation has nothing to do with regular repetition or law. It comes when one *understands* one term (the cause) as *actively producing* the other, as *responsible by its action* for making the other term (the effect) *come to be* (either in whole or in part), so that without the cause in this particular situation the effect would not be. This is an active understanding, not merely a passive reporting of an observation.

The origin of the Greek term for cause (*aitia*) comes originally not from science but from the law courts, where it signified the one *guilty*, or (more generalized) the one *responsible* for something happening.[15] It grew to signify whatever is actively responsible for some given event or entity needing *to be understood* and recognized as not sufficiently intelligible by itself. Thus a causal explanation was not an observation of experience but a *judgment*, based on evidence judged adequate, which assigns active responsibility for an observed event to a *non-observed* cause—not observed, that is, by the judgers, either judge or jury. The notion of efficient cause, therefore, becomes simply a *function of the inquiring mind at work*, and its application just as analogous as the unlimited horizon of this mind and the relevant questions it judges fit to raise. It is, like all metaphysical explanations, an at least implicit commitment to the general principle of the intelligibility (in principle) of all being, tailored to fit the particular situation needing explanation. It can also be expressed as the Principle of Sufficient Reason (though not in the strong rationalist *deductive* sense of Leibniz): whatever is must have the sufficient reason or ground of adequate intelligibility for its existence somewhere in the realm of being, either in itself or in another. But if not in itself, which must first be judged on adequate evidence, then this sufficient reason must be found in another real being, which is called its efficient cause.

Thus there is no artificial restriction built into the meaning or application of the notion of cause at all, a restriction either to regular temporal sequence or to the domain of sensibly experienced or even finite events or entities. *Wherever* the mind judges that something needs a further explanation or grounding of its being, it posits as cause *whatever is needed* to be actively responsible for it, together with whatever attributes are needed by the responsible one in order to fulfill its job description. It is this broadly analogous use of cause and causal explanation that I have been relying on here, and I make no apologies for it, to Kant or to anyone else. This is the fundamental movement of all explanatory metaphysics: that there are "must-be's" (relations of intelligible exigency) woven everywhere into the very fabric of reality which are not merely explications of the *meaning of words*.

In fact, Kant himself is guilty of a fundamental incoherence in his own system of thought because of his refusal to apply causality beyond the realm of sense experience. On the one hand, he insists that the causal relation is an *a priori* category of the mind that can be applied only within the phenomenal domain of given sensory experience. But on the other hand he insists with equal vigor that he is not an idealist, that he holds a real noumenal world of things-in-themselves which *act* upon us, producing our not entirely indeterminate sense experience within us, since we do not create our sense data out of whole cloth but receive it first passively and only then impose our various *a priori* forms of sense and intellect upon it. But this is precisely to do what he says cannot be done: extend the law of causal action and explanation from what is given within experience to something (the source) outside our horizon of experience— namely, the thing-in-itself.

He cannot have it both ways. He must either deny the application of causal explanation beyond experience—then also deny that we can know that any real world is there at all to act on us, that we are *receptive* at all of any kind of given, sense or otherwise—or he must affirm the real world as active source of our sense data and thus extend causality beyond our experience. Yet he denies he is simply an "idealist." He should never have gotten himself into this impossible straightjacket in the first place. And there is no reason for us, 200 years later, to remain within the artificial prison he erected for himself by denying with no good evidence that most fundamental insight of all ancient and medieval metaphysicians as well as everyday practical wisdom—namely, that all action is of its nature revelatory of the nature of its agent-source, even if the latter lies itself beyond the range of our direct experience. Causal explanation, grounded on the principle that all action is the self-revelation of being (also its partial concealment, of course) is but another expression for the mind's radical openness from within the narrow circle of its own inner experience to the vast world of the not-yet-experienced—perhaps never experienceable—surrounding environment of being, insofar as the latter manifests itself as the necessary support and ground of all experience.

The Analogical Structure of Language about God

We have now completed the two basic modes of philosophical discovery of God currently being used by leading Neo-Thomist schools of thought: the inner path through the dynamism of the human spirit toward Infinite Being and Goodness and the cosmic-metaphysical path through participation metaphysics, rising from the many to the One and from the finite to the Infinite, as ultimate Source of all being. Now arises the problem of whether we can say anything more about God than just *that* He is the ultimate Source of all, wrapped in a mystery into which we can penetrate no further. This is the problem which St. Thomas and the medievals treated under the "names of God," which for St. Thomas involves the analogical structure of all our meaningful language about God. There has been a great ongoing dispute in contemporary philosophical circles as to whether language about God, insofar as He is a being beyond our experience, can be meaningful at all, and if so how this is justified.[16] Positivists, empiricists, naturalists, and some types of analytic philosophers deny that language about God or about any transcendent being can be meaningful. They refuse even to discuss arguments for the existence of God: since the very term in question can be given no meaningful content, propositions about "God" are neither true nor false, but simply meaningless. Their basic reason is that all meaningful language about the real world is drawn from a matrix of human experience, and that to use such language to talk about a being beyond our experience and not testable in experience is in principle impossible because it is empty of any content we can understand when applied to such a being.

Nor can the traditional recourse to analogy, as done by Thomists, be of any help, it is said.[17] For an analogous term is defined as partly the same, partly different when applied to different subjects (or analogates, as they say). Hence the term used—e.g., "intelligence"—partly shifts in meaning when applied to God as compared with its meaning when applied to man. But there's the rub. The new meaning that is different because applied to God, precisely because it lies beyond anything we experience, or can test in experience, turns out to be empty. Hence what we can *understand* in the term "intelligence" applies only to *man*, whereas what applies to *God* in its new use we *cannot understand*. Consequently, as applied to God it remains empty and can tell us nothing meaningful.

But even among contemporary religious thinkers—even many Christian thinkers, both philosophers and theologians—analogy, especially of the technical Thomistic kind, has fallen on bad days and is rejected by perhaps a majority, outside Thomists. At least so it seemed to me a few years ago among the philosophers of religion with whom I am acquainted. They do not feel that Thomistic analogy is any real help in solving the problem, either because it remains too formal and empty, too agnostic, or because it is based on a dubious metaphysics they cannot accept. Many of these thinkers, in fact, have abandoned any philosophical attempt to prove or argue at all for the existence of God or His attributes. They have recourse instead to faith or revelation, to suggestive metaphors and symbols or "veridical parables," to existential disclosure experiences (Ian Ramsey, for example) and the like.

I must say that I deeply sympathize with their dissatisfaction with Thomistic analogy as a tool for speaking about God, since I find it a sad fact that it is very difficult to find a good, clear, trustworthy explanation of Thomistic analogy that makes sense to contemporary thinkers and also does justice to St. Thomas's thought. One reason is that around 1960 a rather profound revision of interpretation of analogy in St. Thomas took place among contemporary Thomistic scholars, concomitant with and partly resulting from the rediscovery of the notion of participation and its role in his metaphysics. Thomistic scholars are now generally agreed that it is impossible to find any one consistent theory of analogy that fits all the texts of St. Thomas, that his thought has evolved rather profoundly on this point, and that in particular the doctrine expressed in the early text from the *De Veritate*—which was taken as the paradigm structure for interpreting all the others by the great classical Dominican commentator Cardinal Cajetan, and which has set the style for all the expositions of Thomistic analogy over the last several centuries—was actually quietly abandoned by St. Thomas himself in his later works as too agnostic, to be replaced by a much richer and more metaphysically grounded "analogy of causal participation," as it is now called.[18]

I believe this basic structure of analogical language about God, based on the participation metaphysics which we have presented, can be presented with reasonable clarity and brevity, though there will be many loose ends for further discussion. I would like to attempt this now, drawing heavily on a long article which I wrote for the January 1976 issue of *The Thomist* in reply to a full-dress attack on analogy by Kai Nielsen, the well-known atheist who has written widely on the philosophy of religion.[19] Let us proceed step by step.

Meaning and Use of Analogous Language

An analogous term in general is one which is predicated on several different subjects with a meaning that is partly the same and partly different, as applied to each. Of the various kinds of analogies, we are interested here only in those analogous terms which express literally and properly, not metaphorically or by extrinsic denomination, some real intrinsic similarity found diversely but proportionately in all the analogates. Such analogies are called "analogies of proper proportionality" in traditional Thomistic terminology and are the only ones which are really useful in metaphysics, especially in speaking about God. They include basic terms such as "existence," "goodness," "knowledge," "activity," "unity," "beauty," "power," "love," etc.

Why do we need such analogous terms in our language? We need them in order to express the *real similarities* we discover between different kinds and levels of beings in our experience. These objective real similarities are not in the order of forms or essences, strictly speaking, precisely because they range over many different forms and essences. They are found habitually in the order of activities and of states which can be assimilated to an act or activity in the most general sense. The reason why activity-terms lend themselves to analogous predication, rather than form-terms, is that the same kind of activity can be performed in quite different ways by different agents on different levels of being. Thus power can be exercised by an atom, a plant, a muscle, a mind, or a will; the modes of exercising it can be radically different in each case, yet we notice a genuine similarity, which we wish to express by the unified analogous term "power." Similarly in the case of knowing, in a worm, a dog, or a human being, in both his sense and intellectual activities: the activity is similar, but exercised in a different mode by each subject to which it is applied. Unity and presence, not immediately thought of as activities, are nonetheless best understood as the act of cohering, the act of presence-ing, or presenting oneself, exercised diversely as we run up and down the scale of being.

The importance of this basic principle cannot be overstressed, although it is more often than not never expressed at all in traditional expositions of Thomistic analogy. I state it clearly: all terms expressing a proper analogy of proportional similarity are action-terms, activity-terms, expressing some action or activity that can be exercised diversely by different subjects, proportionate to their natures. Thus even "unity," if carefully analyzed, turns out to be, not a static state, but an active *cohering*, done diversely by different subjects, from material to spiritual.

The next point is that properly analogous terms, at least the great broad ones that are of use to us in metaphysics and speaking about God, are *systematically vague terms*. They elude all attempts to pin them down in a strict definition. They can to some extent be defined negatively in what they exclude, but it is impossible to define them positively save by synonyms equally as broad and vague. Just try defining "unity," for example, as it is found in an atom, a man, a mind, an argument, a family, the universe. Any attempt to do so will at once narrow its range and destroy its usefulness precisely as a flexible concept—a stretch-concept, as I like to call it. How then do we come to know the meaning of such a term? Simply by running up and down the scale of its known examples and seeing the point, catching the point, of the similarity it expresses in all. This is a most important point for the understanding of analogy. A concept or term is not empty or meaningless simply because it cannot be defined. There is an indispensable role played in our thought and language by those systematically vague and elastic terms that alone can catch the similarities and affinities running all up and down and across the universe, especially between the realms of matter and spirit, cosmos and psyche. This is the secret life of the mind nourishing all metaphor, poetry, and art: the insight into authentic similarities and affinities across the universe.

It follows from the above that we cannot properly understand the analogous range of a concept and the partial shift in meaning it undergoes in a particular usage simply by examining the concept by itself. The analogous shift occurs only as the concept (and term) is actually used in the living act of judgment when the mind actually applies it to a given subject and knows what it is doing. No formal analysis of logical structure can capture this dynamic movement, despite all the complicated attempts that have been made, even by such distinguished Thomists as Father Bochenski and James Ross. In my humble opinion all such attempts are fundamentally misguided. Analogy is found and understood only in the *lived use* of concepts and language which takes place in the act of judgment: "This plant has unity"; "This argument has unity." It is beyond all formalism and formal analysis, yet we use analogy quite effortlessly and skillfully many times a day.

How We Extend an Analogous Term beyond our Present Experience

So far we have been examining analogical language to express discovered real similarities within the horizon of our human experience. But we also learn after a while how to extend them beyond to take care of new frontiers of experience or necessary references from within our experience to something outside it. Thus when Freud first found it necessary to postulate the existence of a subconscious and unconscious dimension of cognitive activity in man and extended the term "cognition" to embrace a new level of reality, it is not that he first directly experienced consciously the unconscious, which would obviously be a contradiction, but rather that from new *effects* manifesting themselves in our conscious experience—similar to the effects of other cognitive activities which we already know and which are impossible or unfruitful to explain in completely non-cognitive terms—he concluded to some kind of meaningful similarity between this hidden source of activity and the conscious modes of cognition we already know. He quite spontaneously and legitimately extended the analogous range of the term "knowledge" to include this new postulated dimension of reality beyond the direct reach of our experience. So, too, there is now considerable speculation as to the possible existence of new modes of physical or psychic forces, so-called psi-forces and the like, to account for some of the baffling data of parapsychology, such as precognition, for example. No one knows yet just what they might be like, or whether they exist at all, but we have no trouble extending the analogous notion of "force" or "power" to describe this *possible* new dimension of reality. So too with notions like "rational" and "intelligent." We speculate on the possibilities of contacting some other species of galactic inhabitants, *somehow like ourselves*, but we don't yet know *how*, in what we can meaningfully call their "conscious" life, as Heisenberg has so insightfully remarked.[20]

The general rule is this: whenever the mind finds it rationally necessary or fruitful, either under the anticipation of a possible new dimension of experience or under the pressure of finding necessary conditions of intelligibility outside our experience for what we encounter within our experience, it simply expands its conscious horizon of being as intelligible to open up some new determinate beachhead in the already unlimited, indeterminate horizon of being in which the mind lives implicitly all the time. This is the very nature of the inexhaustible dynamism of the human mind, the root whence all its particular activities flow, as we saw in the first part of this book: that it should be constantly open and seeking to expand its conscious possession of the limitless horizon of being. Thus once the mind has set up a new beachhead of experienced or postulated intelligibility within being, it immediately envelopes it with its own pre-existent and potentially all-embracing field of analogy. If it judges it necessary to save the intelligibility of something in our experience by positing some necessary condition of intelligibility outside our experience, it posits the latter at once as a *real* condition of intelligibility and as *necessarily analogous* with the rest of being, in one and the same movement of thought. From the very beginning of our intellectual life there is a necessary mutual co-involvement of being, intelligibility, and analogy. But as soon as we have found it either necessary or fruitful to expand the application of a particular attribute analogously to some new dimension of reality, we must immediately in the same act *purify* the meaning-content of this analogous term, rendering it less determinate and precise so that its possible range of application will no longer be restricted by its presently experienced range of application. If the term we first pick is resistant to such inner stretching of meaning, we seek for another, broader one which will allow it. This progressive stretching of concepts is going on ceaselessly in our intellectual life, as our experience and our explanatory hypotheses expand.

But it should be noted that analogy is not itself a way of *discovering* anything new, as many mistakenly suppose with respect to the attributes of God. It is the inquiring mind itself that leaps ahead first to establish the new beachhead in being, to whose unrestricted intelligibility it is committed ahead of time by the very nature of its dynamism of intentionality. Analogy comes along only afterwards to *organize* the newly conquered territory and work out the *conceptual* and *linguistic* expression of the bonds of community with the already known. It is a perfectly natural, spontaneous, and valid movement of the mind to extend thus the analogous range of its concepts and language, *provided it has good reason to set up the new beachhead in the first place.* What is this good reason in the case of God?

Extension of Analogous Language to God

As we have seen, we have to have *a good reason* to extend our analogous language all the way to God, understood philosophically as the Fontal Mystery beyond our direct experience. (The language of mysticism has its own logic, which we cannot go into here.) What is this good reason for a Thomist? We are here at the very heart of the authentic Thomistic doctrine of analogy as applied to God—a point consistently missed by many critics. There is only one bridge that enables us to pass over the cognitive abyss between ourselves and God and talk meaningfully about Him in our terms: the bridge of causal participation, or more simply of efficient causality, taken with all its implications. If God were not the ultimate causal Source of all the perfections we find in our world, we would have no way of talking meaningfully about Him at all. It is the causal bond which grounds all analogous predication about God.

What is there in this relation that forges a bond of community between the effects and their cause? It is the fundamental property of all efficient causality—a doctrine implicit in Plato but first laid down by Aristotle, echoed with some reservations by the Neoplatonic tradition, and systematically exploited by St. Thomas in his participation metaphysics— that every effect must in some way resemble its cause. Since all that the effect has comes from its cause and is the gift of the cause, and since the cause cannot give what it does not possess, at least in some higher equivalent way, then under pain of unintelligibility there must be *some* resemblance between the effect and its cause, at least in the most fundamental order of existence and the latter's satellite properties, such as unity.[21] That is precisely why the world, as created by God, has always been considered—and rightly so—as an image of God, imperfect but still participating in its own limited way in the infinite plenitude of the divine perfection.

Creation itself, therefore, immediately sets up a bond of community between the world and God. That is why I find metaphysically unsatisfactory and refuse to use myself the description of God given by some mystics and many religious thinkers, following Rudolf Otto: that God is the "totally Other." I understand what they mean, but I think it is more accurately expressed by saying that God is "infinitely Higher," not "totally Other" than we are. If we took such total otherness at face value, it would sever entirely the bond of community, of connatural affinity, between ourselves and

God. Why then should I wish to be joined in blissful union with something totally lacking any affinity or resemblance with anything in me? Total heterogeneity would allow of no meaningful union. Cut this bond of causal participation between creature and Creator, and all bonds of ontological similarity vanish into the mists; with it all meaningful analogical language about God vanishes too. These may seem hard words for those who have no taste for causal metaphysics in philosophical theology, but I see no alternative for speaking about God, save poetic, metaphorical, symbolic language. This is either going to be empty, excessively anthropomorphic, and without any clear principle of conceptual control, or, if it does indeed turn out to be truly illuminating, as carefully chosen metaphorical language certainly can, it seems to me that it will secretly presuppose the causal bond of similarity through creation as already given. Any metaphor, symbolic image, or story that is not underlaid and supported by some ontological similarity with what it symbolizes evaporates into mere subjective fantasy. Even the language of Revelation, to be meaningful for us who receive it, must presuppose and implicitly build upon the community in being and intelligibility established by the causal bond contained in the notion of creation, even though this may never have been worked out in an explicit technical metaphysics. The core of such causal participation metaphysics is already contained in germ, in fact, in the inexhaustibly rich phrase of *Genesis*, which has nourished so deeply the contemplation and reflection of so many medieval—and modern—mystics and metaphysicians: "Let us *make* man to *our own image* and *likeness.*" I stress the *make*, the *our*, and the *likeness*, the second two flowing from the first.

If there is one point I would like to highlight in this chapter, it is the capital importance of the ontological bond of similitude deriving from causal participation as the indispensable metaphysical underpinning for giving meaning to language about God in Thomistic (and, I do not hesitate to say, I think *any* viable) philosophical theology. It is a source of constant amazement to me how critics of Thomistic analogy, including many Christian thinkers who are good friends of mine, consistently and habitually omit any mention of the metaphysical foundation for analogy when they bring up and discard analogy as an inefficacious tool. All attempts to solve the problem solely by linguistic strategies, Wittgensteinian "forms of life" and so forth, seem to me doomed in principle to failure. Cut the bond of causal similitude between God and creature which, outside direct mystical experience, is our only bridge across the unfathomable abyss between finite and Infinite, and there is no path left to the mystery-shrouded peaks of the farther shore.

Hence the Buddhists are right in not allowing any positive attributes to be applied to God or the Ultimate Reality. For Buddha expressly forbade his disciples to raise any questions about the origin of things, since this would just get them involved in academic disputes and not help them practically to relieve suffering, the main point of his teaching. But once one has removed the bridge of causal similitude between Creator and creatures, there is no way to cross over in our thought or language the abyss between finite and infinite.

Which Attributes Can Be Applied to God?

Once we have set up this basic framework of causal similitude between all creatures and God, from which it follows that there *must* be some appropriate analogous predicates that can be extended properly and legitimately to God, the next step consists in determining just *which* attributes—in addition to ones of existence, infinite perfection, and causal power revealed by the causal argument itself—can allow for open-ended extension all the way up the scale of being, even to the mode of Infinite Plenitude, without losing their unity of meaning. This is the search for the "simple or pure perfections," as St. Thomas calls them, which are purely positive qualitative terms that do not contain as part of their *meaning* any implication of limit or imperfection. Once we have located one of these, even though we enter into its meaning in first discovering it through the limited and imperfect modes belonging to the things we find in our experience, *what we intend or mean* directly by the concept, when we have purified or enlarged it for good reasons into an analogous concept, is a flexible, broadly but not totally indeterminate core of purely positive meaning that transcends all its particular possible modes—both those we know and those we do not know.

We can recognize that we have effected this purification when we can meaningfully affirm, as we certainly do, that *all* the experienced modes of these open-ended perfections, such as unity, knowledge, love, and power, are *limited*, not-yet-perfect modes. For to affix the qualification "limited or imperfect" to any instance of an attribute is already to imply that our understanding of this attribute transcends all the limiting qualifiers we have just added to it. Any attribute that cannot survive this process of purification or negation of all imperfection and limitation in its meaning without some part of its very *meaning* being cancelled out does not possess enough analogical "stretch" to allow its predication of God. The judgment as to when this does or does not happen is of course a delicate one that requires careful critical reflection, along with sensitivity to the existential connotations of the use of the term in a given historical culture.[22]

Two types of attributes have been sifted out as meeting the above requirements by the reflective traditions of metaphysics, religion, and theology: (1) those attributes whose meaning is so closely linked with the meaning and intelligibility of being itself that no real being is conceivable which could lack them and still remain intelligible—i.e., the so-called *absolutely transcendental properties* of being, such as unity, activity, goodness, and power—and (2) the *relatively transcendental properties* of being, which are so purely positive in meaning and so demanding of our unqualified value-approval that, even though they are not co-extensive with all being, any being higher than the level at which they first appear must be judged to possess them—hence *a fortiori* the highest being—under pain of being less perfect than the beings we already know, particularly ourselves: such are knowledge (particularly intellectual knowledge), love, joy, freedom, and personality, at least as understood in Western cultures.

The Absolutely Transcendental Properties

Once established that God exists as supreme, infinitely perfect Source of all being, it follows that every attribute that can be shown to be necessarily attached to or flow from the very intelligibility of the primary attribute of being itself must necessarily be possessed in principle, without any further argument, by this supreme Being, under pain of its not being at all, let alone not being the supreme instance. Thus it is inconceivable that there should exist any being that is not in its own proportionate way *one*, its parts, if any, cohering into one and not dispersed into unrelated multiplicity. Hence God must be supremely one. Such all-pervasive properties of being are few, but charged with value-significance: e.g., unity, intelligibility, activity, power, goodness—in the broadest ontological sense as having some perfection in itself and being good *for* something, if only itself—and probably beauty too.

Since these properties are so general and vague or indeterminate in their content—deliberately so, to allow for their completely open-ended spectrum of application—we derive from this inference no precise idea or representation at all as to what *this mode* of unity and so forth will be like in itself. But we do definitely know this much: *that* this positive qualitative attribute or perfection (in St. Thomas's general metaphysical sense of the term as any positive quality) is really present in God and in the supreme degree possible. Such knowledge, though vague, is richly *value-laden* and is therefore a guide for value-assessment and for value-responses of worship, love, and the like. What we know with certainty is that God must be Number 1 in all these attributes, hence eminently worthy of our unique adoration and veneration.

The Relatively Transcendental Properties

There is a second genre of transcendental attributes of being that are richer in content and of more immediate interest and

relevance in speaking about God. These are terms that express positive qualitative attributes having a floor or lower
limit but no ceiling or upper limit, and hence are understood
to be properties belonging necessarily to any and all beings
above a certain level of perfection. Their range is transcendental indefinitely upward but not downward. Such are
knowledge, consciousness (especially self-consciousness and
intellectual knowledge), love, joy (bliss, happiness—i.e., the
conscious enjoyment of good possessed), and similar derivative properties of personality in the widest purely positive
sense—not the restrictive sense it has in many Oriental traditions. All such attributes reveal themselves to us as "pure
perfections" once—and only if—we come to recognize them
as *totally positive* values in themselves, no matter how imperfectly we happen to possess them here and now. As such,
they demand our *unqualified approval* as unconditionally *better*
to have than not to have. Hence we cannot affirm that any
being that exists higher than ourselves, *a fortiori* the supremely
perfect being that God must be, does not have these perfections in its own appropriate mode. To conceive of some
higher being as, for example, lacking self-consciousness in
some appropriate way—i.e., being simply blacked out in un-
consciousness—would be for us necessarily to conceive this
being as lower in perfection than ourselves. Nor is there any
escape in the well-known ploy that this might merely mean
inconceivable *for* us but in reality might actually be the case,
for all we know. The reason is that to affirm that some states
of affairs *might really* be the case is to declare it in some way
conceivable, at least with nothing militating against its possibility. This we simply cannot do with such purely positive
perfection-concepts.

What happens in our use of the concepts, as soon as we know or suspect for good reasons that there exists some being higher than ourselves, is that even though *our discovery* of their meaning has been from our experience of them in limited degree, we immediately detach them from *restricting* links with our own level, make them more purified and indeterminate in content, and project them upward along an open-ended ascending scale of *value-appreciation*. This is not a logical but an existential move, hooking up the inner understanding of the conceptual tools we use with the radical open-ended dynamism of the intellect itself. One way we can experience this power of projection of perfections or value-attributes beyond our own level is by experiencing reflectively our own poignant awareness of the limitations and imperfection of these attributes as we possess them now, even though we have not yet experienced the existence of higher beings. We all experience keenly the constricting dissatisfaction and restlessness we feel over the slowness—the fuzzy, piecemeal character—of our knowing and our intense longing the further we advance in wisdom for an ideal mode of knowledge beyond our present reach. The very fact that we can judge our present achievement *as limited* and *imperfect* implies that we have reached beyond it by the implicit dynamism of our minds and wills. To know a limit as *limit* is already in principle to have reached beyond it in dynamic intention, though not yet in conceptual representation. This point has for long been abundantly stressed by the whole Transcendental Thomist school, not to mention Hegel and others, who bring out that the radical dynamism of the spirit indefinitely transcends all finite determinate conceptual expressions or temporary stopping places.

The knowledge given by such projective or pointing concepts, expressing analogous attributes open-ended at the top, is again very vague and indeterminate, yet charged with far richer determination and value-content than the more universal transcendental attributes applying to all being, high or low. By grafting the affirmation of these attributes, as necessarily present in their appropriate proportionate mode in God, on to the lived inner dynamism of our spirits longing for ever fuller consciousness, knowledge, love (loving and being loved), joy, and so forth, these open-ended concepts, affirmed in the highest degree possible of God, can serve as very richly charged *value-assessment guides* for our value-responses of adoration, reverence, love, and longing for union.

But note here again that the problem of the extension of analogous concepts beyond the range of our experience cannot be solved by logical or conceptual analysis alone, but only by inserting these concepts into the context of their actual living use within the unlimitedly open-ended, supra-conceptual dynamism of the human spirit (intellect and will) existentially longing for a fullness of realization beyond the reach of all determinate conceptual grasp or representation. Thomistic analogy makes full sense only within such a total notion of the life of the spirit as knowing/loving dynamism. The knowledge given by these analogous concepts applied to God, therefore, though extremely indeterminate, is by no means empty. It is filled in by a powerful cognitive-affective dynamism involving the whole human psyche and spirit, which starts from the highest point we can reach in our own knowing, loving, and joy, from the *best* in us, then proceeds to project upward along the line of progressive ascent from lower levels toward an apex hidden from our vision at the line's end. We give significant meaning to this invisible apex precisely by *situating* it as the apex of a line of unmistakable direction upward. This delivers to us, through the mediation (not representation) of the open-ended analogous concept—an obscure, vector-like, indirect, non-conceptual, but recognizably positive knowledge-through-love—through the very upward movement of the dynamic longing of the spirit toward its own intuitively felt connatural good: a knowledge "through the heart," as Pascal puts it; or through "connatural inclination," as St. Thomas would have it.[23] Such an affective knowledge-through-connatural-inclination is a thoroughly human kind of knowing, quite within the range of our own deeper levels *of experience*, as all lovers and artists (not to mention religious people) know. Yet it is a mode of knowing that has hitherto been much neglected in our contemporary logically and scientifically oriented epistemology.

Conclusion

To sum up, analogous knowledge of God—as understood in its whole supporting metaphysical context of (1) the dynamism of the human spirit, transcending by its intentional thrust all its own limited conceptual products along the way, and (2) the structure of causal participation or causal similitude between God and creatures—delivers a knowledge that is intrinsically and deliberately vague and indeterminate, but at the same time richly positive in content. For such concepts serve as positive signposts, pointing vector-like along an ascending spectrum of ever higher and more fully realized perfection, and can thus fulfill their main role as guides for significant value-responses, both contemplative and practical. Such knowledge, with the analogous terms expressing it, is (and by the nature of the case is supposed to be) a *chiaroscuro* of light and shadow, of revelation and concealment, as Heidegger would say, that alone is appropriate to the luminous Mystery which is in its ultimate object—a Mystery which we at the same time judge that we *must* reasonably affirm, yet whose precise mode of being remains always beyond the reach of our determinate representational images and concepts, but not beyond the *dynamic thrust* of our spirit which can express this intentional reach only through the open-ended flexible concepts and language we call analogous.

Such concepts cannot be considered "empty" save in an inhumanly narrow epistemology. What critics who make this charge consistently and strangely overlook is that, though our analogous knowledge of God does not provide us with any clear mental representation or insight as to the *manner* or way in which God possesses the perfections we attribute to Him for good reasons, what it does do is inform us with unambiguous clarity and precision as to His *rank* on the scale of value and perfection—namely, that He is Number One, the supreme peak in all orders of perfection. It is this knowledge which is, after all, the most essential and fruitful for the principal religious purposes that thought and language about God are called on to serve. Thus for purposes of reverence, worship, love, hope, and longing, it is not necessary for us to know exactly *what* God's wisdom, love, goodness, or power are like in themselves; it is enough to know *that* He is supreme on the scale of these values, and for this *reason* eminently and uniquely *worthy* of our unqualified worship, love, hope, and desire for union with Him. Such luminous precision in the order of value-knowledge is far from empty or sterile: it is life-guiding and life-inspiring in the highest degree.

Could we reasonably ask more of a philosophical knowledge of God?

PART THREE

Christian Theism and Whiteheadian Process Philosophy: Are They Compatible?

There is little doubt that during the last few years the principal challenge to traditional Christian theism has come from Process philosophy and theology, which has continued to show itself as one of the most lively and creative movements in contemporary philosophical and religious thought.[1] A growing number of Catholic thinkers have also been drawing inspiration from the writings of this school.[2] But I have the impression that some of the latter, especially theologians, are a little incautious in speaking of themselves as "Process theologians," or as "using Process philosophy," taking the latter rather vaguely and generally as thinking about God in dynamic terms, without fully realizing all the implications involved in taking on the whole Process philosophical system as such. Hence it seems timely to propose some initial and tentative reflections on just how far Process philosophy and traditional Christian theism— especially as found in the Catholic tradition—are really compatible, or whether there are still some irreducible differences between the two.

Let me begin by summing up briefly the general position I will develop here. On the one hand, Process thought contains a number of *basic insights* that can and should be fruitfully recognized by Christian theism. On the other hand, Process thought *as a system*, at least in its principal presently established forms—the systems of Alfred North Whitehead and Charles Hartshorne—is still in serious tension, if not incompatibility, with traditional Christian theism on several key points, both philosophical and theological, with respect to the nature of God and His relations with the world. It would be unwise, however, to lay down any unbridgeable incompatibilities of principle with future possible developments of the Process stream of thought, since it itself is in full process of evolution, to which it is committed in principle.[3]

A very significant evolution has in fact already taken place. With some notable exceptions, such as Charles Hartshorne, the early Whiteheadian disciples tended to form a closed school interested mainly in the internal creation and clarification of the system rather than in creative adaptations. When confronted with incompatibilities between the system and traditional Christian teaching, many Whiteheadians tended to bend their theology to fit their philosophy rather than adapt their philosophy to their theology, as has always been the hallmark of the great orthodox Christian theologians of the past. Now that the main lines of the system have been tied down with some general consensus, this "scholastic period," as some have called it, is for the most part over. Neo-Whiteheadians are springing up everywhere, especially among Christian theologians and philosophers, who exhibit a new spirit of creative adaptation, even significant revision, of the system where they feel it necessary to fit their Christian belief or human experience. Catholic thinkers can only welcome this trend, since it promises a much more open and creative context for fruitful dialogue to the enrichment of both parties. All that we say hereafter must be understood in this open-ended context of development among sincere Christians who seek to understand their faith.

Is God Creator of the Universe? Whitehead's Position

God is not, in the original Whiteheadian system, the Creator of the universe out of nothing—i.e., out of no pre-existing material or subject.[4] The universe is an ongoing system which has always been and always will be. God does indeed play an indispensable role in this world system, in four ways: (1) as source of the "eternal objects," the possible intelligible forms or structures which He holds eternally in His mind and presents at the appropriate time for integration by the momentary "actual occasions" or events (also called "actual entities"), which alone are real agents outside God Himself; (2) as providing the initial "subjective aim" or ideal goal of each newly arising actual occasion; (3) as providentially guiding the universe toward the greatest possible realizable value, not by determining or coercing creatures through efficient causality, but by "luring" them with the persuasive power of the good;

(4) as eternally preserving in His memory the objectified values achieved by the successively perishing actual entities.

But God is not the ultimate source of the very being of the universe, or even, it seems, of its universal built-in character of self-creativity, for two reasons. In the first place, God's activity always presupposes the universe as somehow already present, at least in inchoate form, as subject of His action, as something He can lure to the good by presenting form and goal, but of which He is not the ultimate source and hence over which He does not possess absolute control. The situation is close to that of the Platonic Demiurge, which injects forms into pre-existing chaotic matter and which Whitehead explicitly recalls as his basic model. Thus he excludes any theory of the absolute beginning of the universe or of any one ultimate source for all reality. A few texts from Whitehead himself will make this clear:

> There is another point in which the organic philosophy [Whitehead's] only repeats Plato. In the *Timaeus*, the origin of the present cosmic epoch is traced back to an aboriginal disorder, chaotic according to our ideals. This is the evolutionary doctrine of the philosophy of organism. Plato's notion has puzzled critics who are obsessed with the Semitic notion of a wholly transcendent God creating out of nothing an accidental universe . . . it is necessary to remind ourselves that this is not the way the world has been described by some of the greatest intellects. Both for Plato and Aristotle the process of the actual world has been conceived as a real incoming of forms into real potentiality, issuing into that real togetherness which is an actual

thing. Also, for the *Timaeus*, the creation of the world is the incoming of a type of order establishing a cosmic epoch. It is not the beginning of matter of fact, but the incoming of a certain type of social order[5] . . . the doctrine of an aboriginal, eminently real, transcendent creator, at whose fiat the world came into being, and whose imposed will it obeys, is the fallacy which has infused tragedy into the histories of Christianity and Mahometanism.[6]

Because God gives the initial subjective aim to each new actual occasion, God can be termed the creator of each temporal actual entity. But the phrase is apt to be misleading by its suggestion that the ultimate creativity of the universe is to be ascribed to God's volition. The true metaphysical position is that God is the aboriginal condition which qualifies its action. . . . But of course there is no meaning to "creativity" apart from its "creatures," and no meaning to "God" apart from the creativity and the "temporal creatures," and no meaning to the temporal creatures apart from "creativity" and "God."[7]

Elsewhere Whitehead adds that we should not pay God the dubious "metaphysical compliment" of being "the foundation for the metaphysical situation with its ultimate activity." For if this were the case, "there can be no alternative except to discern in Him the origin of all evil as well as of all good. He is then the supreme author of the play, and to Him must therefore be ascribed its shortcomings as well as its successes."[8] Thus God is not the ultimate initiator of the cosmic drama with all its players, nor, especially, does He initiate and carry it on by an act of free volition. God and the world are necessary mutual collaborators forever, by the very nature of each: "metaphysics requires that the relationships of God to the world should lie beyond the accidents of will, and that they be founded upon the necessities of the nature of the world."[9]

The *second reason* why Whitehead cannot accept the strict interpretation of creation out of nothing is closely linked with the first. It is because each actual occasion (or actual entity) is a *self-creative act*—not entirely out of nothing, but as a novel autonomous integration of the prior actual occasions in its environment which present themselves to it for selective prehension (these data for decision include God's own presentation of ideal form and goal). "Creativity," which is really self-creativity, is a universal attribute of all actual entities, of which God is the supreme but not the only instance. This concrete act of self-creative integration, which constitutes the very subjective being (= becoming) of each actual occasion, must, insofar as it is a concrete existential act, be *its own* act and not received from another. At best God might be called "co-creator" of each actual occasion, in that He provides the initial subjective aim to guide the entity's own self-creative act. Creativity is not concentrated in God alone, nor does it seem to derive from Him alone (as we shall see, this point might be open to a different interpretation or at least adaptation of Whitehead), but is shared among all actual entities, from the lowest to the highest, and necessarily from the very nature of things, not from any free volition on God's part. As Whitehead puts it,

> In this way an actual entity satisfies Spinoza's notion of substance: it is *causa sui*. The creativity is not an external

agency with its own ulterior purposes. All actual entities share with God this characteristic of self-causation. For this reason every actual entity also shares with God the characteristic of transcending all other actual entities, including God.[10]

And Lewis Ford comments:

> From the standpoint of Christian concerns White-head's metaphysics is most distinctive in that it is a philosophy of creation which does not identify creative power exclusively with God. Instead of distinguishing between a creator who is uncreated and creatures who do not create, Whitehead conceives of all actualities, including God, as self-created. . . . Creativity is the underlying dynamic activity enabling each actuality to create itself, but this creativity is not actual in and of itself, only in its particular instantiations. The role of God is not to supply this creativity but the actuality's ideal of itself (the initial subjective aim) which functions as the principle of selective appropriation of past causes.[11]

Lewis Ford goes on to explain elsewhere, very perceptively, why, according to his mind, Whitehead cannot accept a strict doctrine of divine creation.[12] Take, for example, a free act. It would make sense—say, in a Thomistic system— for God to create *a free agent* which then produced its own free act from within by its own power (supported, if need be, but not determined by God). But this would imply a distinction between subject or agent and act which a White-headian could not accept without going back to the old substance-accident doctrine. For him, there is no distinction between the agent and its act. There is no other being of the free agent save the momentary free act itself. The agent is its act. On the other hand, it would not make sense to say that God created *the free act itself* of another being, for then He Himself would be responsible for the act and it would no longer be the free act of another. Hence, just as the act of any agent must be its own, if it is free, and cannot be given to it ready-made by God or anyone else, so the very being of the free agent for Whitehead, since its being is identical with its act, must be *causa sui* and not given by anyone else, even God—though God can contribute to it and cooperate with it. It follows that in the Whiteheadian system it is impossible for God to create any free agent.

Furthermore, we can push the argument all the way to include all actual entities. For since every actual occasion for Whitehead is a novel, not entirely predetermined act of self-integration, it contains something analogous to freedom within it. Hence none of them could have been created by God. In a word, if all actual entities *are nothing but their acts,* one actual entity for each act, and even God cannot directly create the act, let alone the free act, of another being, then God cannot create any actual entities at all. If God were a creator, He could directly create only agents, not acts. (As we shall see later, there may be another alternative to this neat and tight argument against the possibility of creation for Whitehead, in that he himself carefully limits the meaning of self-creation and distinguishes it from the prior initial constitution of the new subject by the inflow of God and the surrounding world, from which point the creative self-integrating act of the subject then takes off.)

Conflict with the Traditional Christian Notion of Creation

It seems evident enough from all these texts, especially the first set, that Whitehead is quite explicitly and self-consciously rejecting what he understands to be the traditional Christian conception of God as radical ultimate source of the universe, bringing it into being out of nothing in an absolute beginning, by His own free creative act of will. In so doing he is returning to an older Platonic primal dualism of God and the world, in its aspect of primal raw material or multiplicity to be brought from chaos to order—neither of these two poles being ultimately responsible for the origin or total being of the other. The only ultimate source of unity in the universe—if there is one at all (there was none in Plato)—seems to be pushed back even beyond God to an inscrutable, necessary, and eternal amorphous force of "creativity" or self-creativity (of which God is the primary and highest instance, but not, it seems, the ultimate source): a force which carries strong overtones of the ancient Greek *ananke*, or necessity, to which Plato himself appeals. We shall see later how the implicit resources of Whitehead's own system will allow contemporary Neo-Whiteheadians to take quite a different position on this point.

This conception of God's relation to the world falls short of the traditional Judaeo-Christian belief in God as the radical Creator or Ultimate Source of the very being of the universe with all its components—a belief professed clearly by all major Christian creeds: "I believe in one God, the Father almighty, Creator of heaven and earth . . ." From the early Church Fathers down to the present, this has always been interpreted as meaning creation out of nothing (*creatio ex nihilo*)—i.e., initiating the being of the world out of no preexisting subject or matter. It is true that the Biblical texts themselves contain no explicit metaphysical statements such as "creation out of nothing." But the early Fathers, from the second century on, quickly agreed on this interpretation as what distinguished their doctrine from that of the pagans.[13] Thus St. Theophilus of Antioch, writing as early as A.D. 181, explicitly repudiates the doctrine of the "Platonists" that matter itself was not created by God but is eternally coeval with Him as that out of which He made the world:

> But if both God and matter are ungenerated, then God is no longer the creator of all things, according to the Platonists. . . . But the power of God is shown forth in this, that he made out of nothing whatsoever he wished. . . . And so in the first place all the prophets have taught with complete consensus that God created all things out of nothing.[14]

This doctrine was agreed upon so unanimously by all, heretics included, that the early Church councils, directed primarily against Trinitarian and Christological heresies, found no need to explain and define the point explicitly. But in the thirteenth century the resurgence of new forms of Manicheanism brought about a formal definition of the doctrine, in 1215, in the Fourth Lateran Council—an ecumenical one—where God is defined as "Creator of all things, visible and invisible, spiritual and corporeal, who, by his almighty power, from the beginning of time has created both orders in the same way out of nothing, the spiritual or angelic world and the corporeal or visible universe."[15] The same teaching was repeated in later councils, down to the Second Vatican Council in the twentieth century.[16] Thus the doctrine of the initial creation of all things out of nothing is not merely one theological interpretation put forward by some particular theological school or schools, but a basic pillar of orthodox Christian faith, in both Eastern and Western Churches, for all who accept the teaching authority of the Church, unanimous on this point from its earliest days, in both East and West. It should be carefully noted, however, that in no fully authoritative document of the Church (decrees of councils, for example) is there any further determination of what is meant by "from the beginning of time." Whether this positively excludes interpretation in all possible Whiteheadian senses *might* still be open for theological and philosophical discussion.

Metaphysical Difficulties

In addition to being incompatible with traditional Christian belief in God as creator, Whitehead's rejection of an initial creation of the world out of nothing runs into serious metaphysical difficulties. On the one hand, as we have said above, it brings us back to an older Platonic primal dualism of God against the world (in the latter's aspect of primal raw material or multiplicity to be brought from chaos into order), where neither of these two primal poles is ultimately responsible for the other. What then is the ultimate source or explanation of the unity of the universe, of why its two correlative poles, God and the multiplicity of the world, are attuned to each other so as to make up a single system, since neither one ultimately derives all its being from the other? If there is to be any ultimate source of unity in the universe at all—which is dubious, just as it was for Plato—it seems to be pushed back beyond even God to an inscrutable, faceless, amorphous force of creativity which is just *there*, everywhere in the universe, as a primal fact with no further explanation possible—a kind of generalized necessity of nature, with striking similarities to the ancient Greek *ananke*. It should be remembered, too, that creativity for Whitehead is not an actuality in and for itself, but only a generalized abstract description of what is a matter of fact instantiated in every actual occasion of the universe. Creativity seems to be an ultimate primordial *many*, with no unifying source.

But not only is this doctrine in any of its forms not a Christian one, it also suffers from all the irreparable deficiencies of any ultimate dualism or multiplicity not rooted in the prior unity of creative mind. This lacuna in Plato was quickly recognized by the post-Platonic schools of Neoplatonism, culminating in the great synthesis of Plotinus, who considered himself as only completing the unfinished business of Plato by his doctrine of emanation of all reality from the One, including matter itself. Whitehead has turned our metaphysical clocks back not only to a pre-Christian but to a pre-Neoplatonic position, thus cancelling out one of the most decisive metaphysical steps forward in Western thought.

Even aside from the question of how to ground the unity of the system of the universe, with its two intrinsically correlated poles, God and the world, there remains another difficulty: if all creativity does not ultimately derive from God, why does this creativity continue to spring forth endlessly and inexhaustibly, all over the universe, in each new actual occasion, from no actually existing source? For creativity is not, as Lewis Ford insists, an actuality in and of itself, but merely a generalized description of the primal fact that it does spring up in each new actual occasion. It is not itself a source because it is not in itself an already existing concrete actuality. Hence the individual bursts of self-creativity which characterize each newly arising actual entity, and which are the only ground or referent for the term "creativity," seem literally to emerge out of nothing insofar as their actual existence (= *becoming*) is concerned, with no prior ground for their actuality whatsoever—though there is prior ground for their formal elements. Why this creativity should bubble up unfailingly and inexhaustibly all over the universe through endless time, with no active causal influx or gift of *actuality* from another already existing actual entity, remains a total enigma—one that is not simply a mystery to us at present, but in principle rebuffs any further penetration by intelligence, since there is no more ultimate ground.[17]

Lewis Ford, one of the most representative Process thinkers in America, has responded to this objection by stating that once this first step is granted everything else falls into place, and that this is the most one can ask of an initial metaphysical principle. It seems to me, however, that the price of this initial enigma is too high. The doctrine of creativity is admittedly obscure and undeveloped in Whitehead. But until this difficulty is cleared up, the process theory of God remains both theologically and philosophically inadequate to express either the traditional Christian conception of God as creator—i.e., Ultimate Source of the very existence of the universe, as well as of its intelligible structures—or the metaphysical exigencies of an ultimate ground for the unity of the universe. An infinitely fragmented force of creativity cannot be an authentic ultimate, precisely because it is *actually* a many, and only abstractly one.

(To his great credit, however, in his later years, after the first edition of this book, Lewis Ford has suggested that a creative adaptation of Whitehead can be and should be made, according to which God becomes the ultimate Source of all creativity, which he then actively shares with all other beings. This would go far towards healing one of the basic gaps in the internal unity of the system.)

We find ourselves here in the presence of what seems to many of us *the* most radical metaphysical opposition between Whitehead and St. Thomas—and, it seems to me, on St. Thomas's side, most of the great metaphysicians in history, both Eastern and Western. In St. Thomas there is an absolute priority of the One over the many, so that the many is unqualifiedly derivative from and dependent on the One, in an asymmetrical relation. In Whitehead, there is in the last analysis an *original priority of the many over the One.*[18] No matter how much Whiteheadians may insist that the One brings into unity the many—that the One and the many are intrinsically correlative to each other, so that neither is prior to the other—it remains unalterable that the unity of synthesis is *a later or secondary ontological moment* (not necessarily temporal).

The original or primordial ontological contribution of each side of the correlation of God and world is radically and ultimately *independent of the other*. God is not responsible for there being a many at all—i.e., the basic "raw material" for there being a world to be brought into order at all. He is not even responsible for its primordial *potentiality* to be ordered; nor, obviously, is the world responsible for there being a God with the power to order it. This is true even in the primordial nature of God with respect to the infinite set of "eternal objects" or formal pattern-models of order and value which He eternally envisages and draws upon to lure the world into harmony, like the Platonic Demiurge which Whitehead takes as his explicit inspiration. Though the determinate ordering of these pure formal ideal possibilities is due to His creative initiative, still the primordial presence of some quasi-indeterminate reservoir of not yet integrated formal possibilities is not itself generated by the divine creative act but—vague and obscure as its status is in Whitehead— remains an ultimate given of independent origin even for the divine mind and power.[19]

Though this ultimate reservoir of the many in the order of forms does not possess full actual existence as actual entities, still they possess *some* kind of primordial being of their own as their own contribution of raw material for the act of divine ordering into a determinate world of possibilities. Again the many has radical priority, since the duality of God *and* world, God *and* possibles, is itself an ultimate original many. Thus there is no explanation finally of why both sides of this correlation are originally present at all, nor (another serious difficulty often overlooked) is there any reason given why there should be a positive *affinity* of one for the other—i.e., a positive *aptitude or intrinsic capacity* in one to be ordered by the other. Thus neither the *original presence* or givenness of the two sides of the correlation One/many (God/world) nor their *intrinsic tendency and capacity* to mutual correlation is given any explanation or ground. The many—at least in the sense of this initial duality of component terms—retains absolute priority, grounded in no prior or deeper unity.

But practically all of the great metaphysicians of the past, East and West, except Plato and Aristotle, have agreed on at least this: that *every* many must ultimately be grounded in some more primordial and ultimate One. A many makes no sense at all unless there is some common ground or property (existence, goodness, actuality, creativity) shared by each, without which they could not be compared or correlated at all. Nor can any many be intrinsically oriented toward order and synthesis unless some ultimate unitary/ordering mind first creatively thought up within itself this primordial correlation and affinity and implanted it in the many from one source. Not only all actual order, but all ultimate possibility of order must be grounded in a One, and in a Mind. As St. Thomas often put it, following the ancient "Platonic way" (*via Platonica*), "Wherever there is a many possessing some one real common property, there must be some one ultimate source for what the many hold in common; for it cannot be because things are many (not one) that they share something one."[20] Thus either we leave the many and its correlation with the One ultimately ungrounded, with no attempt at intelligible explanation at all, or else we must have recourse to some further hidden ultimate principle of unity. But this would require for Whitehead recourse either to some ultimate inscrutable principle of blind necessity or to some further God hidden behind his God—hardly Whitehead's cup of tea.

In sum, despite Lewis Ford's insistence that the primordiality of the many as co-equal with the One is one of Whitehead's unique new contributions to modern metaphysics,[21] the fact that it is new does not make it viable. In the last analysis, what is missing from Whiteheadian metaphysics is that it remains content with Plato's Demiurge without pushing on to the underlying doctrine of the One or the Good, which Plato himself finally saw had to be the last word and which Plotinus carried all the way to its implicit consequences—the origin of matter from the One.

I am delighted, however, to learn that in these later years, after the publication of the first edition of the present book, Lewis Ford has been more and more willing to concede that creativity is not simply an independent force on its own, but may be said to be an original gift from God to all other beings, thus strengthening the unitary source of the universe. This would be a significant step toward healing the original unreduced dualism of the system and open a more fruitful dialogue with traditional Thomistic metaphysics.

The Response of the Whiteheadians

Process philosophers, especially theologians, are by no means unaware of these difficulties.[22] They are generally willing to admit that the Whiteheadian conception of God as "co-creator" or collaborator with the universe differs significantly from the traditional Christian interpretation. Some conclude that the latter, especially as it includes the notion of an absolute beginning, is a mythological image which should be dropped. Such a response, however, simply wipes out a large part of the unanimous Christian tradition on this point and can hardly be acceptable for orthodox Christians. Others, like John Cobb, wish to push the Process conception closer to the tradition by drawing out the implications of the Whiteheadian doctrine that God alone gives the initial subjective aim to each new actual occasion. Since this constitutes the initial phase of the latter's being/becoming, it might be likened to an initial gift of being, as an overflow from the divine creativity.[23] At least it makes God the indispensable primary initiator of every new entity, the One without whom the universe would not be.

Why could this not be a somewhat new but still orthodox interpretation of the Biblical datum of creation? If it meant that giving the initial subjective aim to each new actual entity includes giving the dynamic thrust or energy to pursue this goal, we might have a more acceptable interpretation. In this case the self-creativity of the created actual occasion would consist only in how it would use the creative energy given it by God to integrate in its own novel way the environment presented it to pursue its subjective aim. But if it meant that God gave only the formal determination of the subjective aim and its drawing power as a final cause or good, but not the actual energy to pursue it, we would still be faced with the emergence out of nothing of the entity's actuality or actual power.

There is, however, another, much more promising line of approach now being advanced by a number of younger Neo-Whiteheadian Christian philosophers and theologians, who propose that there is a positive overflow, an actual causal influx, both from God and from the neighboring perishing actual entities, by which the living current of creativity is passed on before or just as the immediately preceding actual entities pass away. To back this up, appeal is made to Whitehead's too-little-exploited terms such as "transitional creativity," "transference of energy," and "transmission of energy." The "self-creativity" or *causa sui* aspect of the newly arising actual occasion so stressed by Whitehead is in fact limited to what it does with this influx of transitional creativity, how it selects subjectively its own ways of prehending its past. It is here that the transitional creativity, not yet fully subjectivized, passes into concrescent subjective creativity. When this phase is completed and turns into objectification, the concrescent creativity turns again into transitional creativity and is passed on to the next occasion, or rather actively evokes it. The above interpretation is well expressed by one of the younger, creatively independent Neo-Whiteheadian process thinkers, Marjorie Suchocki, then teaching at the Pittsburgh Theological Seminary, in a personal letter to me about her use of the term "evocation" in an article:

> "Evocation" may be my word rather than Whitehead's, but it seems justified to me on the basis of the language he does use: "transmission of energy," "transitional cre-

ativity," "transference of energy," "universe incarnating itself" (that seems a quite active word), and by the whole notion of objectification defined categorically (1.II.xxiv) as the functioning of one entity in the self-creation of another. The completion of concrescent creativity is at the same time the transmission of creativity—each completed occasion acts as an impulse of energy forcing a new concrescence into being. The *causa sui* nature of the new occasion is its own decision as to how it will deal with the past; the selectivity of its prehensions is its own. This selectivity, of course, turns transitional creativity into concrescent creativity; but upon its completion a new impulse of energy is added to the universe, and creativity is transitional once again. If occasions did not function in this evocative way, how is there an account of the origination of prehensive activity as a new occasion at all?

If one rightly claims God's initial aim as the evocative factor, this still substantiates the above, since God is not an exception to the metaphysical principles. In fact, Whitehead expands on the initial aim's creative character by saying that God and world jointly constitute the character of creativity for the initial phase of the novel concrescence. The priority of God's aim is really only practical—that is, the impulses of energy from the past place repetitive demands upon the nascent occasion, creating a cacophony of impulses. God's continuous unification of the world within the divine nature continuously moves new possibilities for harmonies into play; this initial aim does not add to the cacophony; rather, it renders it orderable; hence the priority which is placed on the creativity of the initial aim. . . . So that the transitional creativity of both God and the world evoke the new occasion into being; the selective prehensive activity is the subjective response by which finally the occasion creates itself, utilizing the creative energy of the past. Transition energy is turned to concrescent energy, becoming at its conclusion transitional energy—the many become one and are increased by one, and the rhythmic dance goes on.

This is an admirable statement and in many ways congenial—this part of the system, at least—to a Thomistic metaphysical conception of the active causal influx of both primary and secondary causes on the ongoing production of the world. If this is authentic Whitehead, then there is surely a fruitful basis for metaphysical dialogue. Notice the two key points: (1) the *active causal influx* of actual occasions on each other, which (2) is proposed as the answer to the key metaphysical objection I posed above, put in her own words: "If occasions did not function in this evocative way, *how is there an account of the origination* of prehensive activity as a new occasion at all?" Excellent! A Thomist could hardly do better in identifying the key metaphysical question. But then it seems that we have overturned what has usually been maintained as one of the key metaphysical principles of Whitehead—namely, that there is no *active* causal influx of one actual entity on another in the present and not even strictly from past to present, since, as is well known, the traditional properties of efficient cause and effect are reversed in Whitehead. It is the effect that actively lays hold of the cause, which offers itself passively, as it were, to be assimilated, more in the manner of an Aristotelian material cause.[24]

Many of what we might call the more "classical" White-headian interpreters insist that the denial of active causal influx from one actual entity to another is such a central piece in the Whiteheadian system that it cannot be given up without radically transforming the system into something else. Yet it seems to me—and to many others, including a growing number of Neo-Whiteheadians—that this is precisely one of the two or three weakest points in the whole Whiteheadian metaphysical system, that this is precisely where Whitehead must be adapted, expanded—transformed, if necessary. Dr. Suchocki seems to me entirely on the right track here. It is simply impossible to render intelligible a dynamic universe without a strong role being given to active causal influx— what an Aristotelian or Thomist would call "efficient causality." Perhaps all that Whitehead really meant, or should have meant, is that one actual entity does not actively determine the *inner part* or core of another actual entity that is the latter's own subjective dealing with the creative energy that has been actively given to it by another. This would not preclude, indeed would require, a genuine active influx into the first phase of the new entity—not merely a presentation of form and lure to the good—and from something actually present, not past.

Possibilities of Adaptation within Whitehead Himself

As regards what Whitehead held in his own meager textual developments of the topic and how far they can be pressed to extract a coherent doctrine, the following seems to me to be the case. A selection of texts from the crucial pages of

Process and Reality and of *Adventures in Ideas* will be enough for
our purposes:

> According to the ontological principle there is nothing
> which floats in the world from nowhere. Everything in the
> actual world is referable to some actual entity. It is either
> transmitted from an actual entity in the past, or belongs
> to the subjective aim of the actual entity to whose concres-
> cence it belongs. . . . The subject completes itself during
> the process of concrescence by a self-criticism of its own
> incomplete phases. . . . But the initial stage of its aim is an
> endowment which the subject inherits from the inevitable
> ordering of things, conceptually realized in the nature of
> God. . . . Thus the initial stage of the aim is rooted in the
> nature of God, and its completion depends on the self-
> causation of the subject-superject . . . God . . . is that
> actual entity from which each temporal concrescence re-
> ceives that initial aim from which its self-causation starts.
> That aim determines the initial gradations of relevance of
> eternal objects for conceptual feeling; and constitutes the
> autonomous subject in its primary phase of feelings with
> its initial conceptual valuations, and with its initial physi-
> cal purposes.

If we prefer the phraseology, we can say that God and
the actual world jointly constitute the character of the
creativity for the initial phase of the novel concrescence.
The subject, thus constituted, is the autonomous master
of its own concrescence into subject-superject. . . . The
deterministic efficient causation is the inflow of the actual
world in its own proper character of its own feelings, with

their own intensive strength, felt and reenacted by the novel concrescent subject.[25]

The doctrine of the philosophy of organism is that, however far the sphere of efficient causation be pushed in the determination of components of a concrescence—its data, its emotions, its appreciations, its purposes, its phases of subjective aim—beyond the determination of these components there always remains the final reaction of the self-creative unity of the universe.[26]

An actual entity's own constitution involves that its own activity in self-formation passes into its activity in other-formation.[27]

What can be drawn from these passages? It is clear that the meaning of creativity, which is self-creativity, is precisely delimited. It does not refer to the radical emerging of the new actual occasion or subject out of nothing, but only to the activity by which the new subject, *already constituted* by the inflow of God and the actual world *as partly determined* subject, proceeds to its further autonomous "self-formation" by deciding what to do with its given input, how to restructure it selectively and creatively, in order to become a fully constituted subject. Thus creativity is not the power to emerge into existence or actuality in an unqualified way, but only the power of an initially constituted subject to transform a given multiplicity, a many, into a new unity, a new one.

Creativity is the universal of universals characterizing ultimate matter of fact. It is that ultimate principle by which the many, which are the universe disjunctively, be-

come the one actual occasion, which is the universe con-
junctively. It lies in the nature of things that many enter
into complex unity. The ultimate metaphysical principle
is the advance from disjunction to conjunction, creating a
novel entity other than entities given in disjunction.[28]

What then is to be said of the actual initial "constitution
of the subject" in its initial, partly indeterminate phase, the
point from which its own creativity takes off? What is responsible for this primary constitution of a unique existential
active subject having its own power of creativity? Whitehead
clearly states that this constitution is the result of the inflow
of both God and the prior actual world, an inflow of which
the new occasion must be *a passive recipient* in this initial phase,
since before it there is nothing at all to exercise creative decision. Yet here is where the ambiguity arises.[29] It looks, on
the one hand, as though we are in the presence of a straight-
forward classical productive action, bringing the new subject
into initial existence—a position which an Aristotelian or
Thomist would find quite congenial. On the other hand,
when Whitehead explains more in detail how this constitution takes place, he seems to pull back from what he has said
above, and we are no longer quite so sure that he has a
productive action in mind. For on the one hand, God's action seems, when explicitly described, to consist only in the
presentation of the initial subjective aim or ideal goal of the
new occasion, an action which seems to be in the genre of
constituting only *the final cause* of the new entity, not its *actual
presence* as a new pulse of energy. Moreover, if one strictly
applies Whitehead's own definition of creativity, it does not

seem that such a constitution of another entity in initial existence could be said to come from the creativity of the prior actual entities inflowing their partially determining data to it. For the creativity of an actual occasion consists, properly speaking, only in *its own interior action* of creatively unifying the input presented to it by others, not in the active production of the actuality of something else. Somehow or other the actual appearance of a newly nascent pulse of concrescing energy seems to have slipped through the net of categories without explanation, as a sheer brute fact. But for a metaphysical explanation it is not enough simply to state the fact that new entities actually do arise. This is a mere description, in no way an explanation or rendering the brute fact intelligible. To accept such a mere statement of fact as an ultimate principle is to accept an unintelligible surd as the basis for all subsequent explanation.

Suggested Adaptation of Whitehead

There seems only one viable path open to us. It is to expand the notion of creativity so that it includes not only the aspect Whitehead has explicitly analyzed—i.e., the power to integrate within oneself the data presented by the actual world and God—but also the power actively to evoke new entities and pass on to them a share of one's own power of creativity in its double aspect. Thus creativity would include in it an active-productive-of-another aspect (or, if you wish, evocative-of-another) much like the traditional notion of efficient causality.

This seems to be the line that Marjorie Suchocki and other young Neo-Whiteheadians are now exploring. For example, Elizabeth Kraus, of the Fordham University faculty, proposed in another article that there are two strands or notions of causality in Whitehead which must be combined. One is his better-known and more explicitly developed notion of efficient causality as the reverse of the Aristotelian— i.e., the passive presentation of data or material for active integration by the effect (the new actual occasion). But there is another implicit and undeveloped notion of ordinary commonsense active or productive causality which suddenly surfaces here and there, one which Whitehead simply takes for granted and uses where necessary. This could be called the "overflow aspect" of creativity. Such a notion seems to be implied in a number of the above texts—e.g., when Whitehead speaks of "the transition of creativity," "the constitution of the subject by God and the actual world," and, in the last text especially, "its own activity in self-formation . . . into its activity in other-formation."[30]

Some months after the first draft of this lecture I was delighted to witness exactly the same point being made with striking clarity and vigor, built up carefully from Whitehead's texts, in a brilliant but obviously (from the strong opposition it aroused among the leading Whiteheadian commentators present) highly controversial paper delivered by the Neo-Whiteheadian scholar Jorge Nobo, at the December 1978 meeting of the Society for the Study of Process Philosophies. Nobo's point was that in the total process of the appearance of a new actual entity there are for Whitehead two quite distinct phases: (1) *transition,* the process by which the already constituted and objectified world actively flows over in efficient causality to constitute in being the initial stage of the new subject with its relevant data represented within it (in this phase the new occasion is "other-caused"); and (2) *concrescence* itself, the process by which the now initially constituted subject actively and self-creatively responds to the data given to it to form its own original subjective synthesis (the self-causing or self-creative phase). The consensus of the leading commentators (Leclerc, Christian, Sherburne, Ford) has telescoped the two phases unjustifiably into one, so that transition becomes nothing more than the succession of concrescences, with all the activity condensed into the self-creation of the new actual occasion. Professors Sherburne, Ford, and others who were present, however, objected that Nobo's texts were taken mainly from the early sections of *Process and Reality* and that Whitehead had reversed himself on this point in his last section—a point denied by Nobo.

Whether or not Whitehead had clearly in mind or consistently held onto this other-regarding aspect of creativity, Nobo's analysis makes eminent metaphysical sense to me and fills in beautifully what would otherwise be an obvious and puzzling lacuna in the system. Creativity would thus become a significantly richer notion than usually attributed to Whitehead. Though not an actual entity by itself, apart from its presence (might we not say participation?) in particular concrete actual entities—supremely so in God—it would nonetheless be an actually present power, amorphous and indeterminate in itself but taking on the determinations of whatever actual entity it temporarily inhabits—a power by which each new entity *both* integrates within itself the input of the actual world prior to it *and* also transcends itself by *actively* evoking (or communicating its power to) new actual entities as it itself perishes. Such a notion would bring Whitehead into much closer relation to the whole classical tradition of efficient causality and open up the possibility of more sympathetic dialogue between his system and these other traditions, in particular Thomism.

Such a conception of creativity as an actual causal influx—hence at first *passively received*, for the simple reason that it constitutes the receiver in actuality as the *initial phase* of a *henceforth self-creative* subject—might also open the way to a theory of the radical origin of the universe out of nothing, springing from the primal influx of creativity from God alone, who would not merely lure a previously existing many into increasing and more valuable unity, but would also start off the primal many into the existential adventure of the universe. Once the active evocative power of creativity over others is admitted, I see no intrinsic reason why the Whiteheadian system could not creatively expand its horizon to incorporate the notion of absolute beginning.

I know that Whitehead and Whiteheadians object to allowing this one limit-situation of an absolute beginning, because (among other reasons) it would introduce an exception to the general metaphysical laws by which each new actual entity comes to be in the present ongoing universe— i.e., by creatively selecting and responding to the contribution of previous actual entities.[31] But such laws can only be for Whitehead descriptive of what goes on *now*. This might be enough if all one is intending to do is a *philosophy of nature*, of the internal structure and functioning of the already constituted cosmic system, as Whitehead himself seems to have started off intending to do. But Whitehead was gradually forced to move more and more into the claims of a total metaphysical system, and his present disciples certainly propose his system as an adequate competitor to the great total metaphysical systems before him. Once one accepts the burden of total metaphysical explanation—not merely of descriptive generalization of our limited horizon of present experience—then it seems to me a lack of metaphysical imagination to refuse to make place for the special "limit situations," involving absolute beginnings if necessary. The radical question of absolute origin and unity—i.e., why there actually exists a universe at all and its ultimate source of unity—cannot be dodged by a metaphysician.

With regard to the situation of an absolute beginning, for example, I see no compelling reason why a Whiteheadian as metaphysician should not say that this unique limit-situation is in the nature of the case filled with mystery and beyond the reach of direct description, and that what *must be* (to render the situation intelligible) is that each actual entity in the simultaneously co-created initial state of the cosmic system responds creatively to the only data provided for it: (1) the subjective ideal aim proposed to it by God, who has already taken into account the entire ordered system of ideal aims He proposes to all the other co-created actual entities, and (2) whatever already objectified minimal data, immediately created by God, the first actual entities need to get going. In such a Whiteheadian creationist perspective, all creativity would derive from God as Ultimate Source, but then be shared immanently with all creation as an actually immanent—part actual, part potency-laden—reservoir of energy or power, in itself amorphous, hence not existing as another entity apart by itself, but taking on the determinate form of each new actual entity that it would enter into, and actively flowing over from one to the other as the evocative, creative source not merely of an entity's own subjective act of integration but also of the initial phase of another's. The similarity with the Thomistic act of existence—*esse* or *virtus essendi*, the power of the act of being, as St. Thomas likes to put it—is striking, though from other points of view the two notions are not identical. I see no good reasons (apart from historical ones, which have never deterred metaphysicians) for not expanding or if need be transforming Whitehead along these lines. Such a move would open up promising and fruitful new lines of dialogue between Whiteheadians and Thomists, for example—not to mention other Christian thinkers strictly as metaphysicians. Thomists would still have their problems with the notion of an entity that partially determines its own essence, but this problem might well be contained inside the confines of a strictly philosophical discussion within the general horizon of a shared Christian vision of God as creator, as Ultimate Source of the very coming into being of the universe as a whole.

Reasons behind Whitehead's Refusal of Creation

Just why is it that Whitehead himself seemed so adamant in refusing to explore this possible line of development of his own principles? It seems to me that this arises from a basic misunderstanding, both by himself and by many Whiteheadians following him, of the implications that necessarily follow accepting the traditional doctrine of God as omnipotent creator. In their minds, only two alternatives seem to be open: (1) either one holds that God is the ultimate source of all reality by a free act of creation out of nothing and is thus the source of all power, the omnipotent planner of the world and its destiny (and in this case one must also hold that creatures have no power of their own but are totally determined like puppets in all their actions) or (2) if one wishes to hold that creatures do have power of their own, and can, if free, make their own decisions even against the will of God, then one must also hold that God cannot be an omnipotent, free creator. Thus *either* God is the all-powerful creator, and creatures are powerless, *or* creatures have power of their own, to exercise on their own responsibility, and God cannot be all-powerful creator. Naturally—and wisely, if these are the only alternatives—Whitehead chooses the latter. A similar conception of the traditional doctrine and a similar choice also comes out with unambiguous clarity in the very recent (and in other respects admirable) work of David Griflin[32] —which indicates, I suspect, that it is widely shared among contemporary Whiteheadians.

But such is not at all implied in the traditional position. In Thomistic metaphysics, for example (the general standpoint from which I speak, since I know it best), all creatures participate, as images of God, in the basic perfections of God—*including His power*—although in varying limited degrees, of course. St. Thomas is explicit in rejecting the doctrine of the Arab Occasionalists of his time, according to which *God alone* exercises power and activity, on the *occasion of* the presence of creatures. He insists that to detract from the power of creatures in order to increase the glory of God is in fact to detract from the power and perfection of God, for the more perfect the cause the more of its own perfections it can share, and this precisely shows forth the power of God more perfectly that He shares His power so abundantly with creatures.[33]

To say that God is "all powerful" does not mean that He alone holds and exercises all power, but only that He is the ultimate source of all power and can produce any being or set of beings compatible with His wisdom and goodness. To say that God is the creator of all things does not mean that He directly creates all the *acts* of creatures. God creates *agents*, beings with active natures—or, if you wish, *beings acting*, not *acts*. The proper terminus of creation is not matter or form, acts or accidents, but the whole substantial being with its active powers. The creature, thus endowed with its own intrinsic active power—which makes it also an Aristotelian nature—produces its acts from out of its own power, necessarily or freely, according to its nature. For St. Thomas, God does indeed support or "concur" with the being in its actions. But this divine collaborative power is always channeled through the nature, as root of the act, into the act, and is determined to this or that particular act, not independently and extrinsically by God, but only by the form given it by the determinate nature and whatever use it makes of its powers. The fact that all creatures are totally dependent on God both in their being and in their action does not therefore mean that God *determines* their actions from without. He communicates to creatures their own being and their own native power and supports them in its use, so that without Him they could neither exist nor act. But since He really has given them a share in His own power, they determine the use to which this power is put, even to use it against the express conditional will of God (= *sin*). This is a free self-limitation of God's exercise of His own unlimited power: a self-limitation inherent in every notion of participated perfection and hence part of the very logic of participation.

Thus God does not govern the universe, if He is its creator out of nothing, by "imposing His will absolutely" on creatures from without, as Whitehead seems to believe. The actual carrying out of divine providence (and predestination) can take place very much along the lines that Whitehead and Griffin beautifully describe—by persuasion, by luring to the good—not by coercion. All that an orthodox Christian (even a good Thomist, I would say, according to the basic principles of St. Thomas) must hold today with respect to predestination is that God determines the *general* set of goals *He* wishes to achieve, the goals at which He aims the universe, and knows that in general He will be able to achieve by His suasive power, but does not determine ahead of time in detail just whether or how each particular creature will achieve its share or not in this overall goal. Divine providence unfolds by constant instantaneous "improvisation" of the divine mind and will—from His always *contemporaneous* eternal now—precisely to fit the actual ongoing activities, especially the free ones, of the creaturely players in the world drama. God does not "foresee," from His point of view, anything: He only sees what is going on, and acts accordingly. In a word, *predestination* does not and should not imply total *prede-*

termination. It leaves a large dose of indetermination, to be made determinate—not ahead of time, independently, but only contemporaneous with the actual ongoing development of the world.[34]

My point here, in sum, is this: Whiteheadians and Thomists should not be fighting on the point of divine providence or of the power and freedom of creatures. The Thomistic doctrine of creatures' participation in the power of God, freely granted them by God, plus the distinction between the created agent and its act, is aimed at achieving in its own way the same result as Whiteheadian self-creativity. It is true that in the stricter classical interpretation of Whiteheadian metaphysics one would have difficulty holding both that God is creator and that creatures can freely produce their own acts, since there is no distinction between the agent and its act: the agent is the act, and if God creates the agent, He must create the act itself, which would indeed destroy its freedom. But all this proves is that the *Whiteheadian system* has a difficulty in holding God as creator; it does not warrant attacking traditional Christian theism or Thomism as though they had the same problem. It is Whitehead's problem, not theirs.

But we can go even further. If the interpretation of the Whiteheadian texts on self-creativity which I have suggested earlier is accepted, then he too admits a certain distinction: not only between entities or things, but between phases or aspects of an actual entity—i.e., between (1) the *initial phase* of the new entity as a newly present, already largely determinate nascent "subject," as he calls it, constituted by God and the surrounding world and (2) the immediately subsequent act of self-creative integration by this already inchoately present subject. The notion of self-creation is strictly a limited one, referring only to what the subject does when it "takes off" from its initial *passively received* constitution by another. In a word, there is here too a distinction between agent or subject and act. The difference from the Thomistic theory is not that for Whitehead there is no distinction, but that the act in question is not just one of a successive series in the same subject. Rather, it exhausts the essence and power of the subject in a single act.

But if Whitehead were to follow this line, he too should have no serious difficulty in reconciling divine creation out of nothing with a genuine autonomous power in creatures over their own acts. There is thus a genuine *limited* self-creativity of creatures in the order of action in both Whitehead and St. Thomas—except that for the former the self-creation is said to be in the order of essence, whereas for the latter it is in the order of accidental action, of "self-determination" of one's own action, so that one creatively forms or constructs one's own "accidental" (this does not mean unimportant) psychological and moral personality. Every person as such is, for St. Thomas, *dominus sui*, "master of himself," and thus partly self-creative of his own historical personality. Thomists here are much closer to Whiteheadians than the latter suspect, and the way should be open for more positive dialogue on certain common ground.

Divine Infinity

The second point of tension between the Whiteheadian Process concept and the traditional Christian conception of

God is the question of divine infinity: is the divine perfection truly infinite, and in what respects? As far as the traditional Christian position is concerned, the doctrine of the positive infinity of the divine perfection has been solidly established and universally recognized since at least the fourth century. The term "infinite" itself occurs nowhere explicitly in the Scriptures or in writings of the very early Church Fathers, since it had not yet worked its way into either ordinary or philosophical vocabulary as a positive concept. In classical Greek thought, including both Plato and Aristotle, perfection was habitually identified with the finished, the well-defined or determinate—i.e., the finite or limited—typified by intelligible form. The infinite was identified with the indeterminate, the unfinished, the chaotic, the unintelligible, typified by unformed matter. Even the linguistic term in Greek for perfection came from limit, end (*teleios*, "perfect," from *telos*, "end" or "limit"). It is only with Plotinus and Neoplatonism, as foreshadowed by Philo Judaeus, that the notion of a positive infinity, indicating an excess of perfection *above* all form and not below it, is finally worked out with clear conceptual and metaphysical precision.[35] The first Greek Fathers trained in the Neoplatonic schools at once took it over as the only adequate expression of their belief, and from then on it became the common doctrine of all Christians. It was finally, solemnly defined in the First Vatican Council (1869–70) that God is "infinite in intellect and will and in every perfection."[36]

When we turn to the Whiteheadian God, we must first distinguish between the primordial nature of God, as He is in Himself independent of His relations with the created world, and the consequent nature of God, as He is in terms of the mutual ongoing interchange between Himself and the world. As regards the primordial nature, we shall follow mostly the interpretation of Lewis Ford.[37]

The primordial nature of God, Whitehead says, is infinite. But when the concept is pressed hard, what it finally seems to come down to is only an infinity by extrinsic denomination—i.e., in terms of the infinite number of all intelligible possibilities, each of which is of course finite in itself, which the divine mind thinks up in a single act of primordial envisagement from all eternity. The infinity lies thus on the side of the products of the divine mind, and even here only in their number. But nothing seems to be said of any *intrinsic* infinite fullness of perfection within God's own being in itself. In fact, the primordial nature in itself is said by Whitehead to be "deficient in actuality and unconscious." The reason is that for him all actuality involves a definite, determinate decision, finished off and completed; hence all actuality as such is finite. Whitehead still remains here under the domination of the ancient Platonic notion of the finite as the finished, the perfect—already decisively surpassed by Plotinus. The primordial nature is also "unconscious," because the special meaning of consciousness for Whitehead involves the actual prehending of another actuality. God thus becomes properly conscious only by His actual interchange with the world. It seems, then, that the entire satisfaction and conscious fulfillment of God is an *extroverted* one, absorbed entirely in guiding the world toward intelligibility and value and in treasuring up within Himself the values actually achieved by it in an endlessly ongoing process of mutual enrichment. Here we have a world-dependent God as well as a God-dependent world. And since God is not seen as the actual fullness of all perfection, which He communicates as ultimate source to all creatures in varying finite degrees of participation, His enrichment in the actual order by what He receives from the world is to be taken in a literal and quite strong sense.

If we leave this conception of God undeveloped, as stated above, it is clear that there is quite a gap between it and the traditional Christian theological and metaphysical one of an infinite fullness of God's own intrinsic perfection, of His own inner self-conscious life, quite independently of the world, which He then shares graciously and freely with the world out of the superabundance of His own goodness. Here is where the Christian theological notion of God as Trinity of Persons takes on sharp philosophical relevance. For it illumines how God's own inner life is already rich in infinite self-expression by the Father's total gift of His own being to the Son and the procession of the Holy Spirit from both as their mutual act of love. It is then quite freely—although one might well say *inevitably*, according to the natural "logic" of love—without any need or desire for further self-enrichment, but purely out of the joy of giving that this divine inner life can pour over to share itself with creatures.[38] However, if we admit the creative expansion of the Whiteheadian notion of God to make room for a doctrine of creation as suggested above, I see no insuperable reason why the richness of the traditional notion of the divine infinity cannot also be poured into the admittedly undeveloped Whiteheadian conception of the primordial nature of God. But in order to pull this off successfully, a theory of participation would have to be injected into Whiteheadian metaphysics, according to which the unlimited fullness of an ultimate source is shared diversely in limited degrees by varying finite participants. The apparent absence of such a doctrine casts a puzzling ambiguity over the Whiteheadian metaphysics of God in relation to the world.

With respect to the finitude of the *consequent nature* of God and its constant ongoing enrichment by the response and value-achievements of the world, I would like to treat it in the following chapter, since it is inseparable from the question of the divine relativity and mutability.

God's Real Relatedness to the World, Mutability, and Enrichment by the World

In this chapter I shall deal with the questions of God's relatedness to the world, His mutability, and the resulting finitude of His "consequent nature" (according to Whitehead), since all three are inextricably linked. This chapter is an expansion of my previous paper, "A New Look at the Immutability of God," published in 1972.[39] Continued reflection and discussion with Process thinkers on these problems have led me to a partial rethinking of some of my earlier positions, and on one of them in particular—namely, the real relatedness of God to the world.

There is no doubt that the primary positive contribution of Process thinkers to the philosophical elucidation of the Christian (and any personalist) conception of God has been their notion of God as profoundly involved in and personally responsive to the ongoing events of His creation, in particu-

lar to the conscious life of created persons as expressed in
the mutuality, the mutual giving and receiving, proper to
interpersonal relations. All metaphysical explanations must
make room for these exigencies in any form of personalist
theism. From this Whitehead drew three main consequences:
(1) God is *really related* to the world, especially to persons; (2)
since what happens in the world makes a real difference to
the conscious life of God (for Whitehead, His consequent
nature) and since He is constantly experiencing new joy from
the growth of value in the world and the personal loving
response of His creatures (as well as new compassion for its
disvalues) and newly responding to this, God is constantly
changing in time as the world goes on; (3) because of this, His
consequent nature is finite in perfection. As Hartshorne puts it, at
any one moment God is the supremely perfect Being, surpassed by no other, yet constantly surpassing Himself as He
both gives and receives more from the world. God is *truly
enriched* by the genuine novelty of the ongoing world.

These three conclusions run into headlong opposition to
the traditional Thomistic position that there are no real relations on the part of God toward the world (though there
are, of course, on the part of the world toward God, because
of its dependence on Him), and that God is totally immutable, and not finite in any way in his real perfection or being.
In my earlier article, I tried to mitigate this opposition by
distinguishing between two orders in God: the order of *real
being (esse reale)*—His own intrinsic, real perfection, which remains always an Infinite Plenitude—and the order of *intentional being (esse intentionale)*—i.e., the contents of the divine
field of consciousness as related to creatures. With respect to

the latter—even for St. Thomas, as I tried to show—God's consciousness is certainly contingently *different* in content (in the order of both knowledge and love), corresponding to His decision to create this world rather than that, and also corresponding to what actually happens contingently in the created world, especially the free responses of rational creatures. Thus the world clearly makes a highly significant difference to the conscious, hence personal life of God. And since the divine consciousness as knowing and loving is truly related, by distinct and determinate relations in the intentional order, to creatures—relations based on His distinct ideas of them—it follows, even for St. Thomas, that it is both correct and necessary to say that God is *truly personally* related to the world. Relations in the intentional order are not simply nothing; they are true and authentic relations. But it is also true that in his strict technical terminology and theoretical framework such relations cannot be called "real relations," since all "real" relations for him require that both ends of the relation be real beings in themselves, whereas in the relation of the divine consciousness to creatures only one end is a real being, the creature, and the other is a mental-intentional being which is *about* a real being but not itself another real being.

And it must always be remembered that for St. Thomas, the *difference* in the divine consciousness as intentionally related to particular creatures does not thereby entail any *change* in the divine consciousness, let alone the intrinsic real being of God. For these relations are not first absent at one moment of time and later present at another, but simply present without change in the eternal Now of God. This eternal

Now is itself outside the flow of our motion-dependent time, but present in its own unique time-transcending way to all points of time without internal succession in God. Difference (could have been otherwise, this rather than that) does not logically imply change (*this* after *that*).

God as Really Related to the World

I would now like to make a significant shift of perspective in the above position, with respect to the lack of real relations between God and the world. Can a Thomist say that "God is really related to the world of creatures, and especially to persons endowed with intellect and will"? I think we should be able to use this language, understanding what we are doing and why. We can certainly say, as above, that "God is truly, personally related to his creatures in His intentional consciousness."[40] Within the technical framework of Thomistic terminology, we would also have to add, "but not by what Thomists call 'a real relation,' since this requires that both ends of the relation be real beings, which is not the case here." That is quite true within that technical framework. But I have found over many years of dialogue with modern philosophers outside the Thomistic tradition and most students being introduced to it for the first time that this seems so strange and counter-intuitive to say that God is not really related to us, His creatures; they find it difficult to accept or be intellectually comfortable with this notion. The effort to make this intellectually accessible to them takes more time, with diminishing returns. A widely current looser meaning to the term "really"—that it means little more than "truly"—further complicates understanding. Thus, in current vernacular, to say that "God is not really related to us" is equivalent to saying, "God is not truly related to us at all," which is, of course, false. Hence I would allow such people to say, "Yes, God is really and truly related to us, in His intentional consciousness."

But I present this only as a practical strategy for improved communication in teaching and dialogue with contemporary thinkers outside the Thomistic tradition. It does not at all mean that the traditional doctrine of no real relations between God and the World, especially involving change in God for the Whiteheadians, is false or incorrect. I would still explain to graduate students the traditional doctrine and the reasons for it. Especially I would explain why creation cannot involve a real relation in God to the creature. For when God creates, bestows existence itself on creatures "out of nothing" (no preexisting subject), He is not relating himself to anything real, since there is nothing there yet. He posits in existence the whole other pole of the relation by his own creative act alone. This obviously cannot be a real relation, which requires two real poles to be already there. So let me be clear: I am not proposing a change in Thomistic doctrine itself, but only a realistic strategy for communication with contemporary non-Thomistically trained thinkers. Thus when I tell Whiteheadians that I too am willing to say that God is really related to the world, they are truly delighted, as Hartshorne once told me, that at last he could really talk with a Thomist. And I was able to agree with him that this also meant that if God is related at all, then he is the Sur-related One who is related without exclusiveness to every least creature. But I am not demanding that any other Thomist follow my practical strategy in this matter.

Does this real relatedness of God to the world imply that God is "affected" by what happens in the world, in particular by the response of the love of created persons, so that the personal relation of love between God and man can properly be called a mutual relation, with not only giving but receiving on both sides? This is one of the points that Process thinkers insist on most strongly as alone being able to do justice to the implications of Christian (or any personalist) religious language and to the very nature of interpersonal relations as we understand them more reflectively today.

I would answer—in my project, "creative retrieval of St. Thomas"—that our metaphysics of God must certainly allow us to say that in some real and genuine way God is affected positively by what we do, that He receives love from us and experiences joy *precisely because* of our responses: in a word, that His consciousness is contingently and qualitatively *different* because of what we do.[41] All this difference remains, however, on the level of God's *relational consciousness* and therefore does not involve change, increase or decrease, in the Infinite Plenitude of God's *intrinsic inner being* and perfection—what St. Thomas would call the "absolute" (non-relative) aspect of His perfection. God does not become a more or less perfect being because of the love we return to Him and the joy He experiences thereat (or its absence).

The mutual giving and receiving that is part of God's relational consciousness as knowing and loving what is other than Himself is merely the *appropriate expression* or living out of the intrinsic perfection proper to a perfectly loving *personal being,* the expression of the kind of being He already is. To receive love as a person, as we better understand the unique logic of interpersonal relations today, is not at all an imperfection, but precisely a dimension of the *perfection of personal being* as lovingly responsive. What remains fixed as the constant point of reference in our concept of God is *Infinite Perfection.*

But just what such perfection in fact entails, especially when applied to God as personal, is something that can slowly evolve in *our* consciousness—as the latter itself slowly evolves and deepens in both experience and understanding. Our concept of God is bound to be open to partial evolution as our own understanding evolves as to what it means to be a person, drawn from reflection on our own experience of what it means to be a *human* person, both in relation to other human persons and to God. And if we examine the matter more fully, we realize that God's "receiving" from us, being delighted at our response to His love, is really His original delight in sharing with us in His eternal Now His own original power of loving and infinite goodness which has come back to Him in return. Could we not then possibly agree with the Whiteheadians in saying, in a very carefully qualified way, that God is not only the universe's great Giver, but also thereby its great Appreciator, its great Receiver? This is stretching the language indeed for a Thomist, but perhaps not beyond the bounds of what is really, truly the case?

God as Changing in Time

Does this mean, then, that God undergoes change—is mutable, properly speaking? Does contingent difference in God's relational consciousness necessarily imply change—i.e., temporally successive states in that consciousness? Process thinkers insist on this as one of the key innovations in their concept of God as compared with the traditional Thomistic concept, and as necessarily following from the admission that God is really related to the changing world and positively affected by what happens in it.

My answer here is two-fold. First, it does not follow that contingent *difference* in the divine relational consciousness of the world necessarily involves *temporally successive* states *in God.* I have the impression that Process thinkers tend to move too quickly here, taking for granted without sufficient exploration of other hypotheses that the only way to register in consciousness differences deriving from a changing world is by being immersed in the same kind of time-flow. I do not see how they have ruled out the possibility that the divine consciousness is present to the contingent changing world in a mode of presence that transcends our time-succession.[42] Just because we cannot *imagine* what it would be like to know this is not a reason why it cannot be *thought* and affirmed for metaphysical reasons.

Our kind of time-succession is based principally on the *continuous physical motion* going on in our world and in ourselves which serves as a point of reference for asserting change, a continuous flow of *before* and *after,* subject in principle to measurement. It is therefore based not principally on the pure ordering of contents of consciousness, of "intentional being," but in change in our underlying real, physical, and psychic being. But in God there is only the relational order of the contents of God's intentional consciousness as related to us, without any "moving around" or physical motion inside His own intrinsic being. As to just what God's timeless knowledge of our changing world is like, we have no clear idea and should be more willing than Process thinkers seem to be to leave this as a mystery, not prematurely closing off any metaphysical options.

I have the distinct impression that the Process thinkers I know have never clearly grasped the extremely austere and metaphysically spare meaning of the eternal Now of God's presence to all time-events as proposed by St. Thomas.[43] They tend to conceive of the divine eternal Now as some kind of continuously ongoing time-flow, existing long before—and perhaps after—the present created world, so that God is conceived as knowing the future and responding to it *from* all eternity—i.e., long before it happened. Such a concept would indeed be open to the severe criticism advanced by Process thought. But a Thomist would rather say that God knows and responds to the world not *from* all eternity, but *in* His eternal Now, simply present to each event as it actually takes place.

The key point usually overlooked is that our "nows" *exclude* each other, whereas the divine Now *includes* all others. Hence an equivocation or category mistake is always involved if we attempt to answer questions such as this: "Does God know now (i.e., at 10:00 A.M., August 3, 1978) what will happen on August 3, 1980?" The proper answer should be either "No," or "The question is meaningless, or at least badly put." What we can and should say is simply this: "God *knows* what happens on September 5, 1980, as it happens, for John Smith, or Mary Jones, or anyone you mention, but not for God." But *no time adverb at all,* none of our "nows" or "thens," can be applied to situate His knowledge anywhere in *our* time-sequence. The relationship between His Now and our nows is not expressible in any of our "nows" or time-language. The "No" answer would also be appropriate, since any of our nows *excludes* a future one; hence even God could not know in *one* now *another* now excluded by the first!

It follows in St. Thomas's austere logic of the divine eternity, as pure Presence to that which is, that all questions about divine *fore*knowledge, *pre*destination, and so forth are, properly speaking, false problems, misplaced questions if taken to refer to temporal priority in God. The *mode* of the divine presence is left entirely mysterious. In other words, it is impossible for us ever to *say* in our language *when* God knows anything. Any translation from the all-inclusive Now of God into any of our exclusive "nows" or "whens" is irremediably equivocal. God simply *knows*—period! The consistent overlooking of this key point of the logic of Thomistic God-language by Process thinkers seems to me to vitiate most of their objections to this part of the Thomistic doctrine of God. To see the point can lead to a sudden metaphysical illumination of the Wittgensteinian type: "Whereof one cannot speak, thereof one must be silent."

It is clear, however, that Whitehead cannot accept the above Thomistic doctrine of timeless divine knowledge. The reason is simple. In the primordial nature of God, where there is a certain infinity (indeterminate for Whitehead), there is not yet actual, fully conscious knowledge. This requires determinate (finite) acts of knowledge with respect to our finite world, by successive interactions with our world.

This in turn requires that the divine knower be Himself immersed in the finite time flow of what He knows, so that His treasury of actual conscious knowledge grows steadily through time in tune with the changing world itself. And since God for Whitehead does not already possess the infinite fullness of all perfection in full conscious enjoyment, with a timeless presence to all events in time in His eternal Now, his God must learn of all these events in time from the temporal agents themselves, and also gather up in His memory all the values produced by us in our lives as they occur in time, God also depends on this world itself for His ever-growing knowledge and appreciation of how the world responds to His collaboration. Thus God and the world are always mutually dependent on each other. God can never be truly transcendent of the finite world and consciously infinite in Himself. All this is obviously totally unacceptable to a Thomist, following Aquinas himself.

God's Way of Knowing

All of our discussion about God's knowledge being distinctly different in proportion to our free actions in time may easily give rise to a serious misconception, and already has, not only among Whiteheadians but among many contemporary thinkers outside the Thomistic tradition. It may seem that we creatures, especially free human persons, actually determine God's knowledge by positive causal action on God Himself. This, of course, would make God dependent on His creatures—which would again be totally unacceptable to Thomists. They must, then, explain an alternative way that

God knows the actions, especially the free ones, of His creatures, without positive causal dependence on them.

In fact it does not follow that the only way God knows and receives from creatures is by being acted on physically by them. It is not clear that this even makes any sense in the case of material beings acting on a pure Spirit. The explanation of the way God knows what is done by creatures as I outlined it in the previous paper still, I believe, holds. It is that God is constantly working in and through us with His supportive and collaborative power, supporting both the being and action of every creature. But He allows this transcendent power, becoming immanent within us, to be determinately channeled by the respective natures, especially the free-will decisions of creatures. Thus God knows what we are doing by how we allow His power, in itself superabundantly indeterminate, to flow through us; by how we determinately channel this flow of power, according to our own free initiatives and how we respond to His constant drawing us to our proper good. Thus He knows not by being acted on, but through His own action in us. He knows what we are doing by *doing with us* whatever we are doing, except that it is we who supply the determinations to specify the in-itself-transcendent (and thus indeterminate) fullness of His power. To receive these determinations from creatures is not to be acted upon by them in any proper sense, though the result is determinate knowledge in the divine consciousness.[44]

We might add that the reason why Whitehead himself cannot use such an explanation for divine knowing is that he lacks the resources of a participation doctrine in which creatures truly participate in the divine power, as well as the other perfections of God. For Whitehead, either God has all power and creatures have none, or creatures have their own power to exercise by their own initiative—power which is independent of and against God's own power. In the latter case, of course, if God does receive from creatures it can only be by their acting on Him from without, so to speak. The Thomistic interior symbiosis of divine and creaturely power in every creaturely act avoids the serious problems of this passive and extrinsic conception of divine receiving.

Divine Simplicity

A last but important point. One of the *bêtes noires* of Process thinkers is the Thomistic doctrine of the divine simplicity— namely, that God's being as absolutely infinite must also be absolutely simple, allowing no real composition or multiplicity within it. As Process thinkers such as Hartshorne, Ford, Griffin, and others understand it, it is this doctrine more perhaps than any other which is the villain, rendering void the religious concept of God as involved in mutual loving relations, really related to us, and receiving joy from our responses. Such pure, unqualified simplicity, turning the divine infinity into a motionless, impassive block indifferent to all outside itself, is, they say, an incautious heritage from pagan Neoplatonism, quite alien to personalist Christian thought. Why, after all, should simplicity be put on a higher ontological level than a rich multiplicity?

My answer to this objection contains two parts, beginning with a defense of the Thomistic understanding of this attribute. Against the classical Neoplatonic doctrine of the simplicity of the One, the critique of the Process thinkers is in some respects, I admit, a valid and devastating one. The absolute simplicity of Plotinus's One allowed of no multiplicity, even in the intentional order or the order of relations. Hence all intentional consciousness of the multiplicity of the world had to be relegated to a lower level of divinity, the divine *Nous* or Intelligence, which, as containing a multiplicity of cognitive objects (ideas), was definitely inferior in unity and hence perfection to the ultimate One from which it emanated. There is no place either for an interior Trinity of Persons or for knowledge and love of creatures in such an ultimate and absolutely simple principle.

But Process thinkers fail to recognize the profound transformation that the attribute of divine simplicity has undergone in medieval Christian metaphysical thought, culminating in St. Thomas. The simplicity of the divine being now means only this: that there are no really distinct *ontological parts* making up the absolute divine being in itself. For each such part would involve incompleteness and limitation in itself and would require some higher unitive composing force to unite it with the other parts. But the simplicity thus postulated is restricted to the *absolute* intrinsic being of God. It is *explicitly compatible* with the triple relational distinctness of the three divine Persons—Father, Son, and Holy Spirit—within God. Real multiplicity in the order *of certain relations* does not vitiate simplicity in the absolute (in the technical sense always of "non-relative") being or essence of God, the qualitative perfection of the divine nature as such. Thus when the Father gives His entire identical nature (*what* He is) to the Son in love, and both together to the Holy Spirit, the two

are relationally distinguished as Giver and Receiver, but what
they both possess as their intrinsic perfection of being is the
identical simple and infinite plenitude of *absolute* perfection
that is the divine nature, one nature shared identically by
three giving/receiving Persons. Thus the official Catholic
doctrine, defined in the Councils of the Church and accepted
by all orthodox Catholic theologians, including St. Thomas,
runs thus, in paraphrase: "The only distinction of any kind
between the three Persons in the Trinity is that stemming
from the relation of *origin*, originator-originated, giver-re-
ceiver, not from anything in *what* is given and received, the
identical, intrinsic, infinite fullness of perfection of the absolute divine nature."

Whether one likes, agrees with, or even understands this
doctrine, it is the doctrine taught by St. Thomas and all
traditional Christian metaphysicians. Hence it is clear that
for *them* (though not for Plotinus and his non-Christian fol-
lowers) divine simplicity of *nature* does not exclude real multiplicity in the order of *relations*. As they habitually pointed
out, relation is unique among all the categories in that the
addition of relations to a being does not necessarily add to or
subtract anything from its *absolute* real being and perfection. It
relates the subject to its term but does not necessarily change
or modify it internally in any non-relative way. Thus for one
acorn to be *similar* to another of the same species, or smaller
than one and larger than another, changes nothing in the
inner reality of the acorn: it simply relates it to another. I do
not wish to argue for or defend this doctrine of the Trinity
here—only to make the point that divine simplicity for St.

Thomas remains only in the absolute order of divine being and does not exclude real relational multiplicity.

So much for the first part of my answer, a defense of St. Thomas. I now make another, perhaps significant, concession to my Process friends. I think the simplicity attribute of God has in fact remained too rigid and "simple" in St. Thomas and his tradition. It too needs a loosening-up process of further qualification and distinction similar to what we have proposed for the notions of real relatedness to creatures, namely, distinct multiplicity of content in the divine relational consciousness related to the mental-intentional content of the divine mind and will. As long as multiplicity is confined to the strictly *intentional order* of the divine consciousness as oriented to the created world, I do not see any insuperable difficulty—rather its necessity—in rethinking the interrelated field of meaning of the concepts "infinite," "simple," and "relationally multiple" to allow a rich multiplicity of relations—even real relations, in the looser, broader modern sense of the term—within the infinite internal simplicity (i.e., lack of absolute ontological component parts) of the total divine reality. I am here professing myself ready to open up this new avenue of dialogue, rather than exclude it on some *a priori* metaphysical principle. But since I have not yet had the opportunity to explore it dialogically with others, I can give no more than a tentative commitment to its possibility at present, and assert only that the simplicity of God must be adjusted to whatever is required in order to fit the simplicity proper to the perfection of a *loving personal being*. But I hope that the opening of this door may help to remove one of the most stubborn obstacles to constructive dialogue between Thomists and Process thinkers.

Conclusion

In sum, I have made important concessions to Process thinkers as regards what seems to me to be the core of their valuable contribution to religious-metaphysical thought and language about God: that God can be said in some significant though carefully qualified way to be both (1) *really related* to the world in His intentional consciousness and (2) contingently *different* in his "eternal Now," *because of* what happens in the created world—but all this only in His relational, intentional consciousness with respect to us.

I have insisted, on the other hand, that Process thought both can and should be able to adapt, to assimilate the notion of (1) an *active causal influx* of God on all finite actual entities, such that He can radically constitute their whole initial being in a first radical beginning without needing any independent primordial multiplicity to work on—in a word, a truly creative God from whom all creativity and other perfections flow as from a single ultimate unitary Source, to be freely shared by loving participation with creatures, which then truly have their own intrinsic (though received) power to exercise by their own initiative. This implies the radical and absolute priority of the One over the many, though not the swallowing up of the many in the One; (2) the *actual infinity of the intrinsic reality* of God, already present in His own inner life—made specific by the Christian doctrine of the Trinity of Persons within the divine nature—and not an infinity merely potential or by extrinsic denomination resulting only from thinking up an *infinite number of finite* possibilities. This actual divine infinity can indeed be eternally enriched by creatures in the order of determinate modalities of intentional consciousness, but can never be raised to a higher qualitative level of intensity than the original Source; and (3) that the divine life is entirely outside of any of our (or any) time systems that measure change, in his unique timeless eternal Now, directly present to all events in any changing system "in their presentiality," as Aquinas puts it, as they actually happen; and (4) the divine life takes place outside of all time systems measuring real change, in His own unique eternal Now.

May new light flow in both directions through this sincerely and hopefully opened door!

It is clear, then, that in my judgment the present explicit status of the Whiteheadian conception of God is not compatible in major ways with the traditional Catholic and even with the creatively rethought Thomistic conception. But historians have noted that Whiteheadian Process thought in the United States has passed through a first "scholastic stage" of trying to get clear just what Whitehead himself actually thought. But it has now entered a more creative independent phase of assimilation and rethinking, which may well open new doors of dialogue with an alert and creative Thomism. I have already seen some striking examples of the latter, and hope to see more!

Postscript

Lest there be some misunderstanding that the above difficulties are the only ones that I, as a Thomistic metaphysician, have against the Whiteheadian Process system, let me hasten to add that the above discussion concerns only the *theistic* doctrine of Process thought. Even within this restriction, I have been concerned principally with Whitehead's own position. The distinctive additions to it proposed in Hartshorne's panentheism would require discussion that is far more complicated. Outside the theistic area, the principal (and very serious) difficulty I have with Process thought, both as a metaphysician and a Christian thinker, is what seems to me—and to many even among Process sympathizers—to be the lack of an adequate theory of the perdurance of the concrete individual "I" or "self" through time, with the consequent threat to the assertion of authentic personal immortality. For this is, like creation, a nonnegotiable belief of all streams of Christianity that still remain in contact with their roots. Here, too, Neo-Whiteheadian Process thinkers are busily at work on possible creative adaptations of the original Whiteheadian doctrine to make it more compatible with the exigencies of the most common human experience and of most religious beliefs. A fine example of the creative adaptation of Whitehead is the lecture I heard given by Jorge Nobo a few years ago, suggesting that it was necessary now to add a new basic metaphysical category to those included by Whitehead himself, namely, an "Inegrity," that is, an individual nature and agent that perdured in a self-identity through time, something like the Thomistic substance—not quite the same but fulfilling a similar role!

In conclusion, let me say that the principal reason I have been stimulated, challenged, and influenced by Process thought in general is not so much the particular theses and positions as certain general attitudes, such as the keen sensitivity to the profound interconnectedness and relationality of all things ("Actuality is through and through togetherness") and to God's careful, compassionate watching over and stimulating the creative unfolding and evolution of our world.

NOTES

PART I. THE TURN TO THE INNER WAY IN
CONTEMPORARY NEO-THOMISM

1. See two fine surveys by Gerald A. McCool, SJ, "Twentieth-Century Scholasticism," *Journal of Religion* 58 (supplement 1978): S198–S221; and "The Centenary of *Aeterni Patris*," *Homiletic and Pastoral Review* 79 (1979): 8–15.

2. Cf. the systematic and historical study by Otto Muck, SJ, *The Transcendental Method*, trans. William Seidensticker (New York: Herder and Herder, 1968); and "The Logical Structure of Transcendental Method," *International Philosophical Quarterly* 9 (1969): 342–62. Cf. also Helen James John, *The Thomist Spectrum* (New York: Fordham University Press, 1966); and William L. Beaudin, OFM, "The Philosophy of Religion in Transcendental Thomism," *The Cord* (Siena College) 26 (1976): 172–81.

3. See his *Metaphysics*, trans. Joseph Donceel (New York: Herder and Herder, 1968).

4. See his *Insight* (New York: Philosophical Library, 1956); David Tracy, *The Achievement of Bernard Lonergan* (New York: Herder and Herder, 1970); Hugo Meynell, *Introduction to the Philosophy of Bernard Lonergan* (New York: Barnes and Noble, 1978).

5. See his *Natural Theology* (New York: Sheed and Ward, 1962; revised ed., South Bend, Ind.: University of Notre Dame, 1979).

6. Cf. Muck, op. cit., chapter 10; John B. Reichmann, SJ, "The Transcendental Method and the Psychogenesis of Being," *Thomist* 22 (1968): 449–508; Vernon Bourke, "Esse, Transcendence, Law: Three Phases of Recent Thomism," *Modern Schoolman* 52 (1975–1976): 49–64.

7. See Louis Roberts, *The Achievement of Karl Rahner* (New York: Herder and Herder, 1967); and the special issue on Rahner of *America* 123 (October 31, 1970), especially Joseph Donceel, "Rahner's Argument for God," 340–42. Cf. also the recent magistral synthesis by Rahner himself of the philosophical underpinnings of his theology, *The Foundations of Christian Faith* (New York: Seabury, 1978); and Gerald McCool, *A Rahner Reader* (New York: Seabury, 1975).

8. See the powerful development, just prior to Transcendental Thomism, by Maurice Blondel, in his *L'Action* (Paris, 1893), and the fine paraphrase and commentary by James Somerville, *Total Commitment: Blondel's L'Action, 1893* (Washington, D.C.: Corpus Books, 1968); also John McNeill, *The Blondelian Synthesis* (Leiden: Brill, 1966).

9. *On Truth (De Veritate)*, trans. Robert Mulligan et al. (Chicago: Regnery, 1952), question 22, article 2, response to objection 1. He applies the same notion to the desire of God as the Good. For a modern presentation of the argument for God from the desire of happiness drawn from the texts of St. Thomas, see Umberto degl'Innocenti, OP, "L'argomento 'Ex desiderio beatitudinis' secondo l'Aquinate," *Aquinas* 6 (1963): 207–24; and Stanislaw Kowalczyk, "L'argument eudémologique comme preuve de *Dieu*," *Divus Thomas* (Piacenza) 79 (1976), 185–216.

10. See note 9.

11. I owe this striking image to a comment, during the discussion following the lecture, made by Dr. Beatrice Bruteau of Xavier University, Cincinnati, an old friend and philosophical colleague.

12. Cf. Etienne Gilson, *The Christian Philosophy of St. Augustine* (New York: Random House, 1960); and *The Philosophy of St. Bonaventure* (Paterson, N.J.: St. Anthony Guild, 1965); also the excellent little work of Efrem Bettoni, *St. Bonaventure* (South Bend, Ind.: University of Notre Dame, 1964); Ewert Cousins, ed., *Bonaventure: The Soul's Journey into God* (New York: Paulist, 1978); and *Bonaventure and the Coincidence of Opposites* (Chicago: Franciscan Herald, 1978).

13. Cf. Etienne Gilson, *History of Christian Philosophy in the Middle Ages* (New York: Random House, 1955), 335–38.

14. *The Soul (De Anima)*, trans. James Rowan (St. Louis: Herder, 1949), article 17.

15. *Summa Theologiae*, Blackfriars edition (New York: McGraw-Hill, 1964), Part I, question 12, article 12; question 84, article 7.

PART 2. THE METAPHYSICAL ASCENT TO GOD THROUGH PARTICIPATION AND THE ANALOGICAL STRUCTURE OF OUR LANGUAGE ABOUT GOD

1. They are found in his *Summa Theologiae*, Part I, question 2, article 3. Cf. Edward Sillem, *Ways of Thinking about God* (New York: Sheed and Ward, 1961), for an introduction; and Etienne Gilson, *The Christian Philosophy of St. Thomas Aquinas* (New York: Random House, 1956).

2. *Expositio in S. Joannis Evangelium* (Turin: Marietti, 1952), Prologus; *Summa contra Gentes*, trans. Anton Pegis et al., in *On the Truth of the Catholic Faith* (New York: Doubleday, 1955): Nook III, chapter 38.

3. Cf., e.g., Thomas Connolly, "The Basis for the Third Proof for the Existence of God," *Thomist* 17 (1954): 282–99; Thomas G. Pater, "The Question of the Validity of the Third Way," in *Studies in Philosophy and the History of Philosophy*, ed. John Ryan, 2:137–77 (Washington, D.C.: Catholic University of America, 1963); Toshi-

yuki Miyakawa, "The Value and Meaning of the Third Way of St. Thomas Aquinas," *Aquinas* 6 (1963): 239–95.

4. Cf. Vincent de Couesnongle, OP, "La causalité du maximum: pourquoi S. Thomas a-t-il mal cité Aristotle?" *Revue des sciences philosophiques et théologiques* 38 (1954): 658–80; "Mesure et causalité dans la Quarta Via de S. Thomas," *Revue thomiste* 58 (1958): 244–84.

5. Cf. W. Norris Clarke, SJ, "The Limitation of Act by Potency in St. Thomas: Aristotelianism or Neoplatonism?" *New Scholasticism* 26 (1952): 167–94; "The Meaning of Participation in St. Thomas," *Proceedings of the American Catholic Philosophical Association* 26 (1952): 147–57, with brief bibliography.

6. *Summa Theologiae*, Part I, question 65, article 1, and question 44, article 1; *On Truth*, question 2, article 14; *Summa contra Gentes*, Book II, chapter 15.

7. For the first text, cf. *On the Power of God*, English Dominican translation (Westminster, Md.: Newman, 1952): question 7, article 2, response to objection 9; for the second, *Summa contra Gentes*, Book I, chapter 28.

8. On *Reductio*, cf. the doctoral thesis of my student Astrid O'Brien, "Resolutio in St. Thomas" (Fordham University, 1973).

9. *Commentary on the Metaphysics of Aristotle*, trans. John Rowan (Chicago: Regnery, 1961): Book IV, lesson 17, number 615.

10. Cf. *On the Power of God*, question 3, article 5; *Summa contra Gentes*, Book II, chapter 15, number 3; *Summa Theologiae*, Part I, question 93, article 6.

11. Etienne Gilson, "Pourquoi S. Thomas a critiqué S. Augustin," *Archives d'histoire doctrinale et littéraire du moyen-âge* I (1926): 126.

12. Cf. L. B. Geiger, OP, *La participation dans la philosophie de S. Thomas d'Aquin* (Paris: Vrin, 1942); Cornelio Fabro, *La nozione metafisica di partecipazione secondo S. Tommasso d'Aquino* (Turin: Societa Internazionale Editrice, 1919); Joseph de Finance, SJ, *Etre et agir dans*

la philosophie de S. Thomas, second ed. (Rome: Universita Gregoriana, 1960); and my articles cited in note 5 above.

13. Cf. Peter Strawson, *Individuals* (New York: Doubleday, 1963): xiii; the essays by Strawson and Stuart Hampshire in *The Nature of Metaphysics,* ed. David Pears (New York: St. Martins, 1966); David Kolb, "Ontological Priorities: A Critique of the Announced Goals of Descriptive Metaphysics," *Metaphilosophy* 6 (1975): 238–48.

14. "The Problem of Perception," in *The Philosophy of Perception,* ed. G. J. Warnock (New York: Oxford University, 1967), 62.

15. Hermann Boeder, "Origine et préhistoire de la question philosophique de l'AITION," *Revue des sciences philosophiques et théologiques* 40 (1956) : 421–43.

16. Cf., e.g., Max Charlesworth, *The Problem of Religious Language* (Englewood Cliffs, N.J.: Prentice-Hall, 1974); John Macquarrie, "Religious Language and Recent Analytical Philosophy," *Concilium* 46 (1969): 159–74; my own essays, "How the Philosopher Gives Meaning to Language about God," in *The Idea of God: Philosophical Perspectives,* ed. Edward Madden, 1–27 (Springfield, Ill: Charles Thomas, 1969); and "Analytic Philosophy and Language about God," in *Christian Philosophy and Religious Renewal,* ed. George McLean (Washington, D.C.: Catholic University of America, 1966).

17. Cf. John Morreall, *Analogy and Talk about God: A Critique of Thomism* (Washington, D.C.: University Press of America, 1978). For the agnostic point of view, cf. Kai Nielsen, "Talk of God and the Doctrine of Analogy," *Thomist* 40 (1976): 32–60; my answer to him, "Analogy and the Meaningfulness of Language about God," follows in the same issue, 61–95.

18. Cf. George Klubertanz, SJ, *St. Thomas and Analogy* (Chicago: Loyola University, 1960); Bernard Montagnes, *L'analogie de l'être chez S. Thomas* (Louvain: Nauwelaerts, 1964); Bruno Puntel, *Analogie und Geschichtlichkeit* (Freiburg: Herder, 1970), with valuable historical

summaries of leading authors; Thomas Fay, "Analogy: The Key to Man's Knowledge about God in the Philosophy of St. Thomas," *Divus Thomas* (Piacenza) 76 (1973): 343–64.

19. "Analogy and the Meaningfulness of Language about God: A Reply to Kai Nielsen," *Thomist* 40 (1976): 61–95.

20. Cf. the remarkable expression of this by Werner Heisenberg, *Der Teil und das Ganze* (Munich: Piper, 1972): 288:

Is it entirely meaningless to infer the existence of a 'consciousness' behind the orderly structure of the observable world—these structures being the 'intention' of such a consciousness? Of course, this very question is an anthropomorphization of the problem. For the word 'consciousness' is clearly derived from human experience. So, properly speaking, one should not apply this concept outside the human area. However, if one were to restrict the usage so much, it would be prohibited, for instance, to speak of the consciousness of an animal. Still, one has the feeling that an expression of this kind makes a certain sense. One perceives that the sense of the concept 'consciousness' becomes simultaneously broader and vaguer when we apply it outside the human area.

21. Cf. *Summa contra Gentes*, Book I, chapter 29, number 2, trans. Anton Pegis, in *On the Truth of the Catholic Faith* (New York: Doubleday, 1955):

Effects which fall short of their causes do not agree with them, i.e., are not identical in name and nature. Yet some likeness must be found between them, since it belongs to the nature of action that an agent produces its like, since each thing acts according as it is in act. The form of an effect, therefore, is certainly found in some measure in a transcending cause, but according to another mode and in another way. For this reason the cause is called *an equivocal cause* [St. Thomas is here using the technical Aristotelian term 'equivocal by design,' which is exactly equivalent to St. Thomas's own term 'analogous']. So God gave all things their perfections and thereby is both like and unlike all of them.

See also ibid., Book I, chapter 32, numbers 2 and 7:

> An effect that does not receive a form specifically the same as that through which the agent acts cannot receive according to a univocal predication the name arising from that form. . . . Now the forms of the things that God has made do not measure up to a specific likeness of that divine power; for the things which God has made receive in a divided and particular limited way that which in Him is found in a simple and universal unlimited way. It is evident, then, that nothing can be said univocally of God and other things. . . . For all attributes are predicated of God essentially. . . . But in other things these predicates are made by participation.

See also *Summa Theologiae*, Part I, question 13, article 5.

22. For a fuller development of this point, cf. my two essays cited in note 16 above.

23. Cf. *Summa Theologiae*, Part I, question 1, article 6, response to objection 3; Parts I–II, question 45, article 2. See also Jacques Maritain, "On Knowledge through Connaturality," *Review of Metaphysics* 4 (1950–1951): 483–94; Victor White, "Thomism and Affective Knowledge," *Blackfriars* 25 (1944): 321–28; Anthony Moreno, "The Nature of St. Thomas's Knowledge per *Connaturalitatem*," *Angelicum* 47 (1970): 44–62.

PART 3. CHRISTIAN THEISM AND WHITEHEADIAN PROCESS PHILOSOPHY: ARE THEY COMPATIBLE?

1. This chapter is a follow-up to my previous essay. Here I have both broadened its scope and taken into account some recent

developments in Process philosophy. Cf. "A New Look at the Immutability of God," in *God Knowable and Unknowable*, ed. Robert J. Roth, 43–72 (New York: Fordham University Press, 1973). It is also a significant revision of the same article.

2. Cf. Robert Mellert, *What is Process Theology?* (New York: Paulist, 1975); Ewert Cousins, ed., *Process Theology* (New York: Paulist, 1971); David Brown, Richard James, and Gene Reeves, eds., *Process Philosophy and Christian Thought* (Indianapolis: Bobbs-Merrill, 1971).

3. Cf. the excellent historical survey by Gene Reeves in the collection cited in note 2.

4. Cf. the various essays in the collections cited in note 2. See also the standard studies such as Ivor Leclerc, *Whitehead's Metaphysics* (Bloomington: Indiana University, 1958); William Christian, *An Interpretation of Whitehead's Metaphysics* (New Haven: Yale University, 1959). To me the fullest and most enlightening discussion of creation in Whitehead is Kenneth Thompson's *Whitehead's Philosophy of Religion* (The Hague: Mouton, 1971), chapter 4, where the author defends Whitehead as far as possible, while objectively pointing out lacunae.

5. *Process and Reality* (New York: Harper and Row, 1960), 146–47. For convenience I have (as in my first edition) cited from this edition of *Process and Reality*, since the new definitive text does not differ from the old in the texts I am using. The new text indicates, in brackets, its correspondence to every page of the old.

6. Ibid., 519.

7. Ibid., 343–4.

8. *Science and the Modern World* (New York: Macmillan, 1926), 258.

9. *Adventures in Ideas* (New York: Macmillan, 1933), 215.

10. *Process and Reality*, 339.

11. Lewis Ford, "The Immutable God and Fr. Clarke," *New Scholasticism* 49 (1975): 191.

12. "Can Freedom Be Created?" *Horizons* 4 (1977): 183–88.

13. Rouet de Journel, *Enchiridion Patristicum*, 21st ed. (Rome: Herder, 1951), at *the Index Theologicus*, number 783, for some 38 refer-

ences on *creatio ex nihilo* and the non-eternity of the world and matter.

14. Theophilus of Antioch, *Ad Autolycum*, 2, 4 (*Patrologia Graeca*, 6.1029; Rouet de Journel, number 178). Cf. also Irenaeus, *Adversus Haereses*, 1.22.1 (*Patrologia Graeca*, 7:669; Rouet de Journel, number 194): "We hold the rule of truth, i.e., that there is one omnipotent God who constituted all things through the Word and made them out of what was not." Also the very early text of *Hermas Pastor*, Mandatum 1.1 (*Patrologia Graeca*, 2.913; Rouet de Journel, number 85): "First of all believe that there is one God, who made all things from nothing into being (*ek tou me ontos eis to einai*)." Nothing could be clearer than the later text of St. Augustine, *De Genesi contra Manichaeos*, 1.6.10 (*Patrologia Latina*, 34.178; Rouet de Journel, number 1540): "God is rightly believed to have made all things from nothing, because, although all things formed have been made out of matter, this matter itself has been made entirely out of nothing (*de nihilo omnino*). . . . For we should not be like those who do not believe that the omnipotent God could have made anything out of nothing, since they consider that artisans and other workers cannot fabricate anything unless they have something from which to make it."

15. *The Church Teaches: Documents of the Church* (St. Louis: Herder, 1955), 146.

16. E.g., the Council of Florence (*The Church Teaches*, 148) and the First Vatican Council (*The Church Teaches*, 152). For a similar Protestant Christian view, see Langdon Gilkey, *Maker of Heaven and Earth* (New York: Doubleday, 1965), 42–43: "Almost the entire Christian tradition is in substantial agreement that God brought the finite world into being out of nothing by a 'purposeful' act of His free will."

17. Cf. Edward Pols, *Whitehead's Metaphysics: A Critical Assessment* (Carbondale: Southern Illinois University, 1967), 131.

18. Cf. David Schindler, "Creativity as Ultimate: Reflections on Actuality in Whitehead, Aquinas, Aristotle," *International Philo-*

sophical Quarterly 13 (1973): 161–71; and "Whitehead's Challenge to Thomism on the Problem of God: The Metaphysical Issues," *International Philosophical Quarterly* 19 (1979). The point of the latter article is that for St. Thomas the ultimate common attribute that unites all things, the act of existence (*esse*), is grounded in one actual, concrete source (God), in which it is found subsistent in all its purity and plentitude and from which it flows by participation to all other instances, whereas for Whitehead the ultimate unifying property, creativity, is never found condensed and concretized in one ultimate source, but remains always radically multiple, dispersed among many. See also the important article of Robert Neville, "Whitehead on the One and the Many," *Southern Journal of Philosophy* 7 (1969–70): 387–93.

19. *Process and Reality*, 392: "God does not create eternal objects; for his nature requires them in the same degree that they require him. . . . This is an exemplification of the coherence of the categorical types of existence." Cf. Leclerc, *Whitehead's Metaphysics*, 199; cf. also Kenneth Thompson, *Whitehead's Philosophy of Religion*, 127: "God does not bring creativity into being. . . . Neither does God bring pure possibilities into being. Pure possibilities are named 'eternal objects' precisely because they are uncreated."

20. *On the Power of God*, question 3, article 5; cf. *Summa Theologiae*, Part I, question 44, article 1; Part I, question 65, article 1.

21. Lewis Ford, loc. cit., in note 11.

22. Cf. Gene Reeves and David Brown, "The Historical Development of Process Theology," chapter 2 in *Process Philosophy and Christian Thought*, op. cit., in note 2.

23. Cf. John Cobb, *A Christian Natural Theology* (Philadelphia: Westminster, 1965). See also the careful discussion in chapter 4 of Kenneth Thompson's *Whitehead's Philosophy of Religion*.

24. Cf. Leclerc, *Whitehead's Metaphysics*, 110.

25. *Process and Reality*, 373–74.

26. Ibid., 75.

27. *Adventures in Ideas*, 248.

28. *Process and Reality*, 31–2.

29. See Kenneth Thompson's long and careful discussion in *Whitehead's Philosophy of Religion*, chapter 4.

30. Similar texts are presented by Thompson, *Whitehead's Philosophy of Religion*, 120—e.g., "[Actual occasions, as they perish,] are themselves energizing as the complex origin of each novel occasion" (*Adventures in Ideas*, 356); "The creativity for a creature becomes the creativity with the creature, and thereby passes into another phase of itself. It is now the creativity for a new creature" (*Religion in the Making* [New York: Macmillan, 1926], 92); "In the abstract language here adopted for metaphysical statement, 'passing on' becomes 'creativity,' in the dictionary sense of the verb *creare*, 'to bring forth, beget, produce'" (*Process and Reality*, 324).

31. Cf., for example, Leclerc, *Whitehead's Metaphysics*, 194–95: "But in saying that God is the 'aboriginal instance of creativity,' Whitehead does not mean or imply that God is in the past of all other actualities, in the sense that God was once the sole existing actual entity. A consistent metaphysical pluralism cannot hold that creativity originally had only a single instantiation. Moreover, such a conception of God would constitute a violation of all the categories of Whitehead's system. By the ontological principle and the category of relativity, all actual entities require 'data.' Thus God as an actual entity can no more be without other actual entities than they can be without him."

32. David Griffin, *God, Power and Evil: A Process Theodicy* (Philadelphia: Westminster, 1976). His exposition of St. Thomas is a distressing distortion of the latter's authentic teaching and intention, drawing unwarranted implications from a simplistic and rigid interpretation of his words.

33. *Summa contra Gentes*, Book III, chapter 68 entire, especially numbers 14–15; *On Truth*, question 9, article 2.

34. John Farrelly, *Predestination, Grace and Free Will* (Westminster, Md.: Newman, 1964).

35. For a brief history, see my article, "The Limitation of Act by Potency in St. Thomas: Aristotelianism or Neoplatonism?" *New Scholasticism* 26 (1952): 167–94; also "Infinity in Plotinus," *Gregorianum* 40 (1959): 75–98.

36. *The Church Teaches*, 355.

37. See the important dialogue between Lewis Ford and William Hill, OP, "In What Sense Is God Infinite?" *Thomist* 42 (1978): 1–27.

38. Ewert Cousins makes this point cogently in his "God as Dynamic in Bonaventure and Contemporary Thought," *Proceedings of the American Catholic Philosophical Association* 48 (1974): 136–48. See also Anthony Kelly, "Trinity and Process: The Relevance of the Christian Confession," *Theological Studies* 31 (1970): 393–414.

39. See note 1.

40. There has been a remarkable convergence among recent Thomists toward toning down St. Thomas's doctrine on the real relation between God and the world. Most do not go quite as far as I go here, but try to show how, while not denying the strict words of St. Thomas, one can loosen their interpretation and enrich his doctrine by saying much more than he does—for example, that God is "truly personally related" to the world. See Anthony Kelly, "God: How Near a Relation?" *Thomist* 34 (1970): 191–229; William Hill, "Does the World Make a Difference to God?" *Thomist* 38 (1974): 148–64; idem, "Does God Know the Future? Aquinas and Some Modern Theologians," *Theological Studies* 36 (1975): 3–18; and John Wright's superb scholarly study, "Divine Knowledge and Human Freedom: The God Who Dialogues," *Theological Studies* 38 (1977): 450–77.

41. Hence I formally reject Lewis Ford's interpretation of my position in "The Immutable God and Fr. Clarke," *New Scholasticism* 49 (1975): 194, where he says, "First, it is clear that the contents of God's intentional consciousness are not derived from the external world." In my original essay, and again in this one, I assert

exactly the opposite—namely, that God's knowledge of the actions of creatures, especially their free actions, is due to them, determined by them, hence derived from them. This occurs, however, not by their physically acting on God, but rather by His acting *with* them. This special *mode* of His knowing will be discussed presently.

42. See on this point the penetrating critique of Hartshorne by Merold Westphal, "Temporality and Finitude in Hartshorne's Theism," *Review of Metaphysics* 19 (1966): 550–64, and the discussion of it in *Process Philosophy and Christian Thought*, op. cit., 44–6.

43. Cf. John Wright, art. cit., in note 40.

44. After finishing this article my attention was called to a book by a distinguished German Catholic theologian on the mutability of God as background for a future Christology. The author develops the same point that the immutability attributed to God must be that proper to a perfect *personal* being—i.e., an *immutable intention* to love and save us, which intention then includes all the adaptations and responses necessary to carry this intention through in personal dialogue with us. Thus *personal* immutability includes relational mutability. See Heribert Mühlen, *Die Veränderlichkeit Gottes als Horizont einer zukünftigen Christologie* (Münster: Aschendorff, 1969).

60249320R00099

Made in the USA
Lexington, KY
01 February 2017